B   Dwight, Allan
Put

      Soldier and patriot

PUTNAM, ISRAEL GEN.

SOLDIER AND PATRIOT:

THE LIFE OF

GENERAL ISRAEL PUTNAM

For Allan

Soldier and Patriot:

The Life of

General Israel Putnam

by ALLAN DWIGHT

IVES WASHBURN, INC.

NEW YORK

IVES WASHBURN, INC., *Publishers*
750 Third Avenue, New York, 17, N.Y. 10017

SOLDIER AND PATRIOT: THE LIFE OF GENERAL ISRAEL PUTNAM

LIBRARY OF CONGRESS CATALOG CARD NUMBER: 65-22019
MANUFACTURED IN THE UNITED STATES OF AMERICA

AUTHOR'S NOTE

It would be impossible to write of Israel Putnam if his aide and friend, Major David Humphreys, had not visited him for several months, after he left the service, and taken down the General's own account of his experiences. Humphreys said later Putnam remembered everything in detail, but was more modest about his deeds than his friends or foes. All biographies depend on this first publication. Those of the nineteenth century were largely repetitions of it. In 1902 W. E. Livingston brought out the longest and most thorough account. But even he could not fill some gaps. Daniel, the General's son, before he died burned his father's personal correspondence (according to one account, because he was ashamed of his father's spelling) and also the diary he himself had kept for fifty years. So not much can be found on Putnam's personal life and family. Most of his official correspondence and Orders are in the various collections.

Anyone writing of the French and Indian wars must be grateful to Francis Parkman for his colorful, careful, and exciting history, to the O'Callaghan collection of New York documents, and to the contemporary accounts of Mante, Entick, Knox, and Rogers. For the Revolution, Freeman's vast biography of Washington was instructive; the Peter Force volumes and the many recent collections of eyewitness accounts of the war were helpful, as were many specialized books, such as Bolton's *The Private Soldier Under Washington*. Johnston's *The Campaign of 1776 on Long Island* and *The Battle of Harlem Heights* were invaluable, also Stryker's *The Battles of Trenton and Princeton* and, for an over-all view of Bunker Hill, Thomas Fleming's most readable *Now We Are Enemies*. Many other accounts and biographies contributed to background and understanding of the events and times.

Table of Contents

Chapter One

Why They Called Him "Wolf" Putnam

ABOUT HALF PAST NINE on the morning of September 8, 1755, Colonel Whiting's regiment of provincial troops marched south from the English camp on Lake George in the Province of New York. They were going to meet a French war party. An advance company under Colonel Williams, of Massachusetts, with 200 newly painted Mohawks in the van, had left an hour earlier.

With Colonel Whiting's regiment marched Private Israel Putnam, a stocky, strong man, of middle height, with curly brown hair, wide blue eyes, and a round firm chin set in a broad face. He had been among the first in Connecticut to enlist when the New England legislatures called for volunteers for the army that would drive the French from their forts on Lake Champlain in northern New York. For too many years the French and Canadians and their Indian allies had spread from these forts to raid the border settlements in New England and New York. At last the colonies, with England's help, were

I

going to take the offensive and fight for their lands, their people, and their future. Most of the soldiers, Putnam among them, had never before faced an enemy in battle.

During the previous night two Indian scouts and then an escaped wagoner had reported that a company of French, of size unknown, had passed by the camp on the lake and was heading toward the recently built Fort Lyman. In a Council of War, at dawn, General William Johnson had decided to send 500 men south to find the enemy and another 500 north to cut off their retreat.

Wise old Chief Hendrick, the Mohawk sachem, had picked up one stick and broken it. Then he had picked up five sticks and shown they could not be broken. General Johnson had nodded and agreed that the two detachments should march south together.

Hendrick had shaken his head. "If they are to be killed they are too many. If they are to fight they are too few."

But the General was sure the French were probably only a small party after scalps and plunder and could be easily killed or captured.

Bowing to the man who was his general and his good and trusted friend, Hendrick had gone to make a speech to his warriors that would put them in the mood for fighting. He was old and very heavy, and he had gratefully accepted Johnson's own horse to ride, since he could not march. So, resplendent in paint and a bright red coat, the Chief had set out, followed by his braves and watched by the entire camp. Captain Williams had followed with his regiment, and then Colonel Whiting. No scouts were sent out ahead of the column or to steal through the woods on either side to search for signs of the French.

Three miles from the lake the road entered a narrow,

thickly wooded valley. On the left a brook ran through a steep gorge; on the right rose a straight side of a mountain. The Mohawks were well into the valley when there came a single shot. Then gunfire burst in rows of flames from the forest on both sides and from the road ahead. The Indians scattered. The advance line of soldiers collapsed like rows of cornstalks. The men who were not hit began to run back up the road. Above the shots and shouts rose Williams's voice calling to his soldiers to follow him to a nearby hillock. Heedless, the terrified soldiers raced toward the second regiment. Colonel Whiting shouted to his men to advance and support the few soldiers still firing into the woods. But an even more intense fire opened from the right flank on the crowded, struggling mass of men on the narrow road. There were far too many French and Indians for just a scouting party; obviously a full-scale attack on the English had been planned.

Pressed back by the men who were fleeing, and catching their panic, the whole Provincial column began to retreat. Now Whiting shouted to his men to take cover. Many had already found a rock or a tree from which to shoot. This was Putnam's first engagement, but neither he nor others needed to be told that the running men must be covered, the pursuing enemy held back as long as possible. So while frightened men streamed up the road to the camp, others, firing, reloading, slipping back to another tree or bush, and firing again, kept the French and Canadians and Indians from following too closely. Some Mohawks joined the Provincials, calling to each other that Hendrick had been killed and must be avenged. At last, half a mile from the lake, after one heavy volley, the

French halted and the Provincials and Indians pelted behind the line of tree trunks, flat-bottomed scows, and wagons that had been thrown together at the sound of the firing.

"A very handsome retreat!" bellowed Seth Pomeroy, blacksmith of Northampton, as the last men came through the makeshift gate.

The French would attack soon. Five hundred men were sent outside the camp to fire on the enemy from the flanks. Inside, the Massachusetts men took the right of the line, the Connecticut the left. They were hardly in place before the lines of white-uniformed soldiers came marching steadily up the road. Canadians and Indians suddenly erupted from the forest and hillsides and raced to the improvised defenses. The first attack was against the left and center. Inexperienced though they were, the Provincials held steady, firing rapidly and accurately. The Canadians and Indians melted away to leave the fighting to the regulars. Before the steady fire the regulars drew back. They turned to the right and advanced purposefully. They would take the defenses by bayonet. But the Provincials rose to meet them in hand-to-hand fighting. Again the soldiers were forced back, but again they came on. Suddenly, late in the afternoon, the French could be felt to waver. The Canadians and Indians stopped shooting and began to slip to the rear. Slowly, then more quickly, Johnson's men climbed over the scows and wagons. The French regulars broke as these men, most of whom had never fought in anger before that morning, rushed at them with hatchets and guns swinging like clubs. The French fled.

This Battle of Lake George was Israel Putnam's initiation into war. His commission as second lieutenant was already on its way from Connecticut. Within two months he would be captain of a company of Rangers, and four years later he would be lieutenant colonel of the Connecticut troops. In 1775 he would be one of the first four major generals commissioned by the Continental Congress and the only one chosen unanimously. Who was Israel Putnam, and how did he come to be fighting the French that bright morning beside Lake George?

In 1641 his great-grandfather, John Putnam, with his wife and children journeyed from Buckinghamshire in England to the new lands of Massachusetts. This in itself took courage, for the voyage in the small crowded ships was long, slow, and dangerous, and all would be utterly strange in the new world. But John Putnam obtained a grant of land in Salem Village, built a house, and made a farm and raised his family. His son, Thomas, had a son, Joseph, who inherited the family farm and there brought his bride in 1690.

Joseph showed his own independence and courage two years later when Salem began its hunt for witches. He disapproved of the hunt, and the trials, and said so, and withdrew as far as possible from the people of the village and their hysteria. A sermon was preached against him; his half-brothers stormed at him; his friends argued angrily, ignored him, or threatened him. For six months he kept his firelock loaded beside his chair in his house and a horse saddled in the stable in case friends, relatives, or town officials should come to arrest him. They never did, and when the hysteria died away they came to apologize to him. He forgave them as quickly as he had been

5

quick to stand against them. Friends said later that his warm sympathy for all persons in need or in trouble, his generosity, and his indomitable spirit were all handed on to his son Israel. Joseph's wife came from the same kind of people, with the same courage and independence and sense of duty and responsibility. Her father had been a soldier, a judge, and a member of the legislature of the colony.

Israel, the twelfth child of Joseph and Elizabeth Porter Putnam, was born on January 7, 1718. He was five when his father died, and nine when his mother married again and moved to Salem. Israel stayed on at Salem Village, which was renamed Danvers, with his brother David, who took charge of the farm.

School terms were short in Salem Village, and books were few. Israel spent what time could be spared from farm work and school in the woods and fields. He learned to shoot as soon as he could hold a flintlock and to fish when he could dangle a hook, and loved the outdoor life. Since he was strong and fearless, he soon became the village champion at racing, leaping, and wrestling. And because he was kind and fair and friendly, he was a favorite with all the boys.

One morning he and some friends were wandering through the woods looking for bird nests. Israel spied a handsome one high in a big oak and instantly climbed from branch to branch. As he stretched out his hand for the nest, the branch on which he was standing broke, and he fell, head downward. Half way down, the broken end of a branch caught at the back of his pantaloons. It held, and he was hanging, head down. The boys on the ground gazed upward, horrified.

"Get out your gun, Jim," Israel said calmly, "and shoot this branch that holds me."

Though he was a crack shot, Jim clutched his firelock and backed away. "I'm not much of a shot," he protested. "Likely I'd shoot you 'stead of the branch."

"You won't hit me if you take good aim. There's no time to go for an ax. If you don't shoot through the branch I'll be dead before a half hour's out."

One of the smaller boys began to cry.

"Go ahead," Israel ordered. "Shoot, now, Jim."

Jim backed away. "Guess you're right." He dropped a bullet and wad down the barrel and some powder in the firing pan. Slowly he took aim and fired. The branch cracked and Israel fell to the ground. When he could get to his feet he nodded. "Knew you could do it. Thanks, Jim."

The next morning Israel went back and got the bird nest.

He took pride in his strength and ability to work, and before he was eighteen he was as good as any man in the fields or forests. Sometimes his imagination and courage showed him how to solve unusual problems.

One day a neighbor's big bull turned wild during its summer stay in a large field and could not be caught. The farmer called in his neighbors to help him get the animal to the barn. The men could corner it, but not one dared to try to put a rope around the sharp horns. Israel watched them a few minutes, went to his house, and came back wearing his spurs.

"Crowd him back to the corner of the stone wall," he directed. "Let me see what I can do."

Gradually the stamping, bellowing bull was pushed

7

back into the corner by the circle of pitchforks and rakes. It lowered its head, pawed the ground, and prepared to charge. In one leap from the top of the stone wall Israel was astride the broad back, his spurs digging at the animal's flanks. As it jerked up its head in surprise, Israel seized hold of the curving horns.

"Clear the way!" he shouted.

The men climbed over the wall. The bull raced across the field, its head held implacably high, the spurs steadily jabbing at its sides. Three times around the field it raced, humping and jerking to throw off the thing on its back. Israel stayed on. The fourth time around he called again, "Open the gate!"

As the gate swung back he steered the bull through it.

"It'll be the end of them both," shrieked the farmer.

"Naw," said a man, "Israel's smart. We better follow."

The sound of heavy hooves and thrashing branches led them half a mile through the woods to a small swamp. The bull, its sides heaving, was standing quietly up to its neck in black swamp water. Israel was still sitting on its back.

"He's all right now," said Israel, and he swung the horns toward the path. The bull ambled peacefully to the stable.

Salem Village proudly told the countryside the tale and proclaimed that no other man had ever ridden an angry bull to a standstill.

In 1739 Israel married Hannah Pope and with money from the sale of his share of the farm bought some land in a district called "Mortlake." Twelve years later he moved to Pomfret in eastern Connecticut, and in two years he had paid off the mortgage. The land was fertile and he worked hard, planting and harvesting his crops, planting and grafting fruit trees and introducing new varieties, increasing his flocks and herds. Soon his farm was very prosperous.

In later years Israel was often called "Old Wolf" Putnam, not only as a tribute to his courage, persistence, and wisdom, but because of another unusual exploit in the winter of 1743.

By this time he had large flocks of sheep and goats. There were still wolves roaming the forests between the villages, and farmers set traps for them to protect their livestock. One big old wolf had been caught but had managed to wrench its foot free and escape. It became recognized by its tracks and well-known because it was too wily to be caught again. Now it lurked around Pomfret, killing animals ferociously and wantonly where before it had killed only to eat.

One frosty morning Israel found seventy of his sheep and goats lying dead, their throats mangled by the wolf. Other farmers had lost many sheep recently. So he met with five Pomfret men at the tavern and they agreed on a continuous hunt, to be carried on in pairs, until the wolf was found and killed. A light snow had fallen and the tracks, leading clearly from the Putnam farm, showed the wolf was the one who limped. All that day the men followed the tracks as far west as the Connecticut River. When it grew dark they made torches and followed the tracks back eastward. At daylight hounds were brought to follow the trail. Shortly after sunup a boy lookout saw the wolf disappear into a den of rocks. The weary hunters arrived to find the hounds in a circle outside the entrance. More men drifted down from farms and the village.

First the hounds, good hunting dogs, were sent into the den. After a lot of frantic barks, snarls, and yelps, they hurried out, frightened and bleeding from the claws and teeth of the wolf. Nothing could make them go into the den again. Straw and sulphur were brought from the village, along with food and ale for the men, and burning wads of straw were pushed down the passageway. But the wolf did not come out. Various schemes were tried all day, but without any success. At last, at ten that night, Israel said he would go after the wolf himself.

"It's too dangerous," protested one man. "She'll tear you to bits."

"You'll never get near her," said another. "Den's too small for you."

"It's now or never," Israel told them. "We must destroy the wolf or she will kill all my flocks—and yours. Fetch me a long rope."

When the rope was brought he tied it loosely around his legs. "Now, boys, when I jerk the rope you pull me out." Taking off his coat and waistcoat, holding a torch made of twisted strips of birch bark, he got down on hands and knees and crawled into the passage in the rocks.

Two feet wide, wet and slippery with melting ice, it dipped down for 15 feet, straightened for 10, and rose to a small den. Israel crawled forward until, ahead, at the top of the rise, he saw the wolf's eyes shining in the light of the torch. He kicked the rope and was pulled back so fast his shirt was pulled over his head. He loaded his musket with nine buckshot and took a fresh torch in his left hand and crawled back into the passage and down the slope and to the last rise. Snarling, head lowered, the wolf crouched to spring. Israel fired, kicked, and again was pulled back by the rope. Outside he drank some ale and waited for the smoke to clear away. Then he crawled down a third time. The wolf was there, but when he touched her nose with his torch she did not move. Dropping the torch, he seized her ears and he and the wolf were drawn out by the excited men. The she-wolf was carried to a house a mile away and hung by the barn for all to see. A "wolf jubilee" was held there for the rest of the night.

The story of the wolf hunt spread through New England and made the name Israel Putnam known in all the northern colonies as a man who was afraid of nothing.

He fitted the picture of the fearless hunter and leader. Though not tall, he was very erect and moved quickly and soundlessly. His expression was usually good-humored and lively, but it could become stern, and when his blue eyes grew hard, men obeyed. He always loved a good story, a good joke, a good laugh. His eyesight and hearing were unusually keen. Though he sometimes stammered when talking, his voice could turn strong and commanding, and when giving orders the stammer disappeared and his voice rolled like thunder. He was immensely kind and generous. He never held a grudge or had an envious thought. He made decisions and then acted on them quickly. He was courageous—it was said later that he dared to lead where others dared to follow —but his heart melted at the sight of someone in trouble, and he could not watch anyone suffering without suffering himself. Sometimes he fainted at the sight of blood. In forest warfare he was cautious, wily, persistent, and dauntless. He had immense energy and endurance. Duty was to him an active word, an obligation a man owed to his God, his country, his church, his family and neighbors.

During the 12 years that followed the wolf hunt, Israel worked at developing his farm into the most profitable of the countryside. He built a new house and took an active part in church and town affairs.

In 1755 began the Seven Years' War between England and France, the war called "the French and Indian" in the Western hemisphere. For a hundred years the border settlements of the colonies of New York and New England had been harassed by raids of the French and their Indian allies from Canada. The French were determined to keep the English colonies small and their settlements from spreading west from the seacoast. Coming down through miles of forests, raiding parties burned villages, killed or captured men, women, and children, and often ambushed pursuing militia. Too often a man left his cabin, his family, his farm to join in pursuit of raiders and returned to find the cabin burned, his wife scalped, his children lying with their brains dashed out. Even a stockaded town such as Deerfield in western Massachusetts had been attacked and its people massacred or taken away into captivity in Canada.

Now England was fighting France in Europe. Another place she could strike at the ancient enemy was the colony of New France, which spread along the St. Lawrence River to the Great Lakes. Four expeditions were organized by the British and the colonies. One was against the French in Acadia, a colony on the east coast of Canada;

one against Fort Niagara on Lake Ontario; one, under General Braddock, against Fort Duquesne in western Pennsylvania; one against Crown Point, the fortress on Lake Champlain in New York that had long served as a base for the roving bands that attacked the northern colonies. A call went out through New England for volunteers. Israel Putnam went to Hartford to enlist. It meant leaving the management of his farm to his wife and sons, Israel, fifteen, Daniel, thirteen. But at last a concerted effort would be made to protect the colonies. So, a farmer and a good citizen, Israel Putnam went forth to do his duty as a soldier.

Chapter Two

The Ranger at Lake George

LAKE CHAMPLAIN IS a long slender finger reaching
south from Canada into New York. A little to the east is
a line of massive high hills called the Green Mountains;
to the west the towering peaks of the Adirondacks carry
the eye up and inland until the mountains fade into blue
distance. The Richelieu River carries the lake waters
north to the St. Lawrence. It was near the shores of this
lake that Samuel Champlain, the explorer, claiming all
the lands drained by the St. Lawrence for France, met a
band of Iroquois Indians. They had never seen a white
man and were wary but not hostile. Champlain had as
guides some Algonquins, traditional enemy of the Iroquois; at their urging, and because of a misunderstand-
ing, he shot and killed two of the Iroquois. The Five Nations hated the French implacably thereafter and their
undying enmity made them friends with the Dutch and
English and kept the people of Canada from moving

south to settle. Those two shots changed the future of a continent.

Into the southern end of Lake Champlain tumbles a 15-mile stream, the outlet of Lake George, which is another, smaller lake penetrating still farther south between steep, thickly forested mountains. For years there had been just two French forts on Champlain, Crown Point on the west shore, stone-walled and impregnable, and Fort Ticonderoga at the southern end where the outlet enters from Lake George. Now there was a third: Fort William Henry, a square of log walls, inadequate and incomplete, built under General Johnson at the southernmost tip of Lake George. From here a wagon road ran south past the small Fort Edward to Albany and the Hudson River. All supplies for the troops at Fort William Henry came plodding in wagon trains up this road, so it was a favorite target for French raiders.

The forests on the mountains around Lake George were tall, but beneath their high branches grew often impassable thickets of new growth, or bushes, or immense tangles of fallen trees that blocked sight and passage. Up and down these mountains and through woods moved the Indians and scouts of the French. Surprise in border warfare was vital, either for a quick raid on work parties or supply trains or for a full-scale attack on a fort. The French had known this for years. It took the attack on the camp at Lake George to impress this need on General William Johnson.

On that September afternoon in 1755 General Phineas Lyman of Massachusetts, second in command of the expedition against Ticonderoga, urged an immediate pursuit of the retreating French. They could be harassed, he said, their boats and supplies discovered and destroyed and an English attack on the fort mounted immediately. Johnson flatly refused. He said his men were exhausted by battle, although 500 had been held inactive all day to protect the boats on the shore. Johnson was slightly wounded, jealous of Lyman and unwilling for him to gain any glory, and afraid of another French attack. He put the soldiers to building first a breastwork for defense and then a fort. Recruits from New England arrived daily, but in spite of orders from Governor Shirley of Massachusetts, his superior, that he should attack Ticonderoga, General Johnson refused to move.

Late in September a man named Robert Rogers arrived with other volunteers from New Hampshire. He was tall and strong, brave yet cautious, and wise in woodcraft. His lieutenant, John Stark, came with him. General Johnson sent Rogers with three volunteers to reconnoiter the fort at Crown Point, the army there, and the land between. Rogers brought back a description of the fort and camp, and an estimate of the number of men. From this scouting venture was born the company of Rangers, volunteers under the command of Rogers, which Israel Putnam quickly joined. Within a month he was captain of his own company of Provincial Rangers.

These Rangers were used for scouting and harassing the enemy. They were independent of the army, and only the generals could give them orders. They had to be strong and ingenious men who could make long marches and endure every kind of privation and hardship and be able to outwit the scouts of the enemy. They knew woods lore and understood Indian warfare, and if they did not already know this they learned quickly in order to survive. Armed with gun, hatchet, and knife, carrying a wooden canteen and a blanket, their uniform at first was nondescript, a deerskin hunting shirt and trousers. Rogers wrote out some general rules for them, based on his own experiences, and added that there were a thousand occurrences and circumstances that might make other stratagems necessary "in which cases, every man's reason and judgement must be his guide, according to the particular situation and nature of things: and that he may do this to advantage he should keep in mind a maxim never to be departed from by a commander, viz: to preserve a firmness and presence of mind on every occasion." Their orders were to venture near hostile strongholds and surprise straggling parties and take prisoners, so as to obtain more information, and "from time to time" to "use their best endeavors to distress the French and their allies by sacking, burning and destroying their houses, barns, barracks, canoes, battoes, etc., and by killing their cattle of every kind; and at all times to endeavor to waylay, attack and destroy their convoys of provisions by land and water in any part of the country where they could find them."

Putnam began his Ranger service by saving the life of Robert Rogers on one of their first scouts together. With three other men they sailed in a birchbark canoe 25 miles down Lake George, landed, hid the canoe, and made their way through the forest to Crown Point. From the mountain slope above they watched the men and the fort for a whole day. The next morning they went back to some farms south of Lake Champlain and here, in a barn filled with wheat, the three men were left, while Rogers and Putnam went back to the fort to try to capture a prisoner. Crawling through the underbrush, hiding behind rocks and trees, they worked to within 60 rods of the walls and there spent the night. In the morning they moved yet nearer to the walls. Suddenly a stout Frenchman came out of the gate toward them. Rogers ran to him, leveled his musket at the man's chest, and ordered him to surrender. The Frenchman jumped back and drew his knife. Rogers's musket missed fire. The Frenchman shouted to the sentry at the fort and started for Rogers. Putnam sprinted to the two men, clubbed the Frenchman's head with his musket—there had been no time to load and fire—and he and Rogers raced down the road to the trees and safety. Then, gathering in the three men from the barn, they all returned to Fort William Henry to report to General Johnson.

William Johnson had come as a boy to New York, and by the aid of his wealthy uncle and hard work and astute trading on his own part, had acquired vast lands and a fine house in the Mohawk Valley in central New York. He was the friend of the Iroquois, the Five Nations, and knew how they felt and thought and could influence them as could no other white man. A hearty Irishman, he could dance a war dance all night with the warriors, share their prodigious feasts, and by an eloquent three-hour oration arouse them to fight the French. He was to be made Indian Agent for New York and a Baronet by King George as a result of the defeat of the French at the Battle of Lake George. The Mohawks, the nation of the Iroquois who lived in the eastern portion of the Mohawk Valley, were particularly devoted to him, and they taught the Rangers much of Indian ways in war and in the woods. But even they were always sent out with white officers or soldiers to keep them from forgetting their mission and going off to find new scalps and to be sure the information brought back was accurate. The French also had a number of different tribes as allies, some devoted to particular French leaders under whom they could be effective and ferocious in raids. Baron Dieskau, the French commander, complained that they drove him and his officers crazy with their constant demands for food and brandy and their refusal to go out as scouts unless they felt in the mood. Because the Indians were unreliable, both commanders depended more and more throughout the war on their Rangers for information.

Each expedition, large or small, was called a "scout," and was an adventure, but each was reported matter-of-factly and briefly. Here is how Putnam reported one in October. Like many others, he spelled phonetically, the way the spoken word sounded to him.

REPORT OF CAPT. PUTNAM.
Sent by Capt. Rodgers as a Spy to Tionderogo.

Octr. 9th 1755. Then lift Capt. Rogers upon a neck of Land upon the west side of Lake George and set out towards tycondorogue to see what Discoveries we Could make and after we had marchd about 7 or 8 miles we came upon a Large Mountain near the Heither end of the narrows, and when we came there we Could make no Discovery at all but after sometime wee espyed three Barke Cannoes Drew upon the Shore upon a point of Land that Ran into the Lake, and then wee espyed two Indians Comeing out of the Bushes toward the Cannoes, after water, and after sometime we espyed several french and Indians on the East side of the Lake and soon after that we heard the noise of Cutting, hewing, adsing, and sawing, as tho there was a Large Company of men at work, and by their talking and Laughing their was amongst them, and then we Espyed about thirty Indians Came out of the Bushes on the west side of the Lake on the point within a large musket shot of us, and played a spell on the Beach and then Returned into the Bush, and from the point Eastward, their was almost a Continual fireing and barking of Doggs and talking so we thot it was not safe to proceed to Tycondarogue and so Concluded to tarry there all knight and see what further Discoveries wee Could make by the fires in the knight, and just at Dusk of the evening their Came four Cannoes from the East and went to the west side of the Lake and landed on the point where the others were incamped, and Drew up their Cannoes on ye Shore and by this time wee began to Discover the fires on the point and on the East side of the Lake, but Could not Discover what number their was, because the Bushes were so thick by the Lake but as near as we Could best Judge we thot there was six or seven hundred by the fires and Guards set on both sides the Lake and about Day Brake, they mustered their men to work and then wee Left the mountain and Returned to Capt Rogers on the point and when we Came within sixty or seventy Rods of the point we Espyed thirteen Indians pass by within ten Rods of us, towards the point where we left Capt Rogers, and after they had passed by us, we came to the point where we left Capt Rogers, and found all well this is the Chief of the Discovery and best account that I am able to give.

Israel Putnam.

To Capt Rodgers
  The Report of Captain Putnen.

A long arm of Lake Champlain stretches east of Lake George behind a range of mountains, ending in South Bay nearly two thirds down the lake. Coming from yet farther south, Wood Creek meanders around hills and through forests and empties into South Bay. Both Wood Creek and South Bay were often used by the French for their raids because troops could be transported more quickly, easily and silently by water than through the forests and over mountains, and by using Wood Creek they could land well below Fort William Henry.

Only a few days after Putnam's report, word came in that a small body of raiders had left Ticonderoga and was heading south. Putnam and Lieutenant Robert Durkee hurried north to reconnoiter. At dusk they had still not found the raiders, so they pushed ahead. Then, in pitch dark, they rounded a hill at a place called the Ovens and saw a glow of a fire. They dropped to their knees, flattened out, and, separated by several yards, inched their way forward, peering in the flickering light for the sentries. When the English and Provincials made camp in the woods, and felt secure enough to build fires, the fires were on the perimeter. The men slept within the ring they made: the sentries stood nearby, outside the glow. Slowly, faces to the ground, Putnam and Durkee pushed forward. Not a movement of twig or leaf betrayed their passing. At last Putnam raised his head. The group of fires was so small it could not surround more than a few men. But he was too close to the fires for comfort. He stopped. Ahead was a long low mound. He lowered his head and peered through the dim light. On both sides of him were other mounds. One moved. They were not mounds but sleeping men, 20 of them. He found Durkee's face, white in the light, and risked raising one hand to point backward and began to inch away. But it was more difficult to crawl backward silently. A leaf rustled, a twig snapped. "Halte!" and a shot came simultaneously from a sentry.

Putnam and Durkee jumped to their feet and headed for the welcoming blackness of the forest. Behind them more sentries fired. The two men were still temporarily blinded by the glow from the fires and for a few minutes blundered into bushes and trees. Shots came whistling through the woods. Durkee gave a gasp, but his footsteps never faltered. Putnam swerved around a looming tree trunk, zigzagged and ran on. Suddenly his feet went out from under him, and he plummeted to the bottom of a pit. When he recovered his breath and felt the walls he found they were of smooth clay. A body fell on top of him. Putnam jerked out his tomahawk while his left hand sought for the head of the intruder.

"Are you all right, Captain?" gasped Durkee.

"Aye," muttered Putnam, "but you nearly weren't. Climb on my shoulders and we'll get out of this. There are some rock ledges nearby."

He led the way to the ledges, and the two spent the night rolled up behind a fallen pine tree. In the morning they found that Durkee had been hit in the shoulder, both canteens were pierced by bullets, and there were 14 holes in Putnam's blanket roll. They returned to the fort with news of the scouting party, which was then attacked. The French retired to Ticonderoga.

November was raw and cold. As most of the recruits wore summer clothing, they began to suffer and hence to grumble. It rained and snowed, and water stood in the tents and food was scarce. At length it was decided by the last of several councils to scatter the army, but to leave some from each province to guard the two forts. Among the number who were assigned to Fort Edward was Putnam, and he was so popular with the Provincials he easily persuaded some of the men from Pomfret to stay with him for the dreary months of winter duty. He spent the time scouting and helping to strengthen the forts, which kept deteriorating because they were made for the most part of wood and dirt. In May the Connecticut Assembly relieved him from service and voted him 50 Spanish milled dollars for "extraordinary services in ranging and scouting during the winter past and for annoyance of the enemy near Crown Point."

Putnam returned home for a month and in June was back at Half Moon camp on the Hudson River above Albany. Because the campaign of the previous summer had accomplished nothing against the French forts, a new campaign was planned. Again the New England colonies had gone into debt to raise more men than Governor Shirley, the commander, had requested, providing their men were used only to attack Ticonderoga and Crown Point. To bring in recruits, a bounty of six dollars was offered for enlistment for the campaign, or for a year, and an extra two dollars was added if the volunteer brought his own musket. Each of the provinces supplied powder horn, bullet pouch, blanket, knapsack, and wooden bottle for water. Since the men of a company often came from the same town or area, most of them knew each other and, in practice, chose their own officers, usually as inexperienced and untrained as themselves. Transport for supplies was always a problem, and often the soldiers were short of food, clothing, and ammunition because of various delays of the oxen-drawn wagon trains.

The army moved north, half the troops staying at Fort Edward and half advancing to Fort William Henry. Both forts were constantly harassed by small parties of French and Indians: they crept from the woods to attack sentries, work parties, and wagon trains; they killed or scalped when possible; or they captured men to take back to Canada for information, to sell, or to hold for redeeming or exchange.

A mysterious tragedy was troubling Fort Edward when Putnam arrived. Every morning the sentry at one special outpost to the east was found missing by his relief. Orders were given to challenge three times at any sound of an approach and if there was no answer to fire. But no shots were heard at night, and each morning the sentry had vanished. Three of the bravest men volunteered in succession, and each disappeared. Now only men who were drafted would take the duty at that post. But Putnam volunteered.

That evening while there was still daylight he went over the place and the land around with the greatest care and then settled himself with his back against a large tree to wait. Daylight turned to dusk; dusk deepened into blackness. There were no sounds but the night noises of the forest. At last, well past midnight, he heard one faint crackle in some dried grass to the left. Again all was silent. But something low and black seemed to be lying where there had been not even a shadow before. He looked away for a moment and then looked back. Though there had been no sound, the black thing was nearer. A third glance showed it was still closer to him. Putnam aimed, challenged, fired. The dying echo of the crash was followed by a faint groan. Tomahawk in hand, he crept to the black mass. Under a bearskin lay a dead Indian. After that no more sentries disappeared.

The summer wore away. Each army strengthened its forts, but each commander was unwilling to attack the other. The Rangers of the English, and the Canadian partisans and Indians on the side of the French, were out constantly, watching for any hostile move of the enemy. Sometimes Putnam and his men were with Robert Rogers and his Rangers, sometimes they scouted on their own.

The fighting that involved the largest number of men grew from a successful French attack on a wagon train of baggage and provisions between the two English forts. The French retreated to their boats in South Bay. Rogers and Putnam were sent with 100 Rangers and two "wall pieces" and two "blunderbusses" up the lake to intercept them. At the northern end the two forces met, and a number of boats of the French were sunk and a number of the raiders killed. But the survivors raced to Ticonderoga with word that the Rangers were at hand and could be trapped. That night the French commander sent 300 men in boats up Lake George to intercept, in turn, the Rangers as they moved south. The next morning the two forces fought a naval battle of maneuver, advance and retreat, with each side trying to ram the other's boats. But the wall pieces and blunderbusses, with their larger shot, tore holes in the bark canoes and cut swathes through the men crowded in the bateaux, which made the boats overturn. After an hour the French withdrew, and the English boats swept triumphantly home.

In October, one of Putnam's scouts was particularly admired. Six men in a whaleboat rowed halfway down Lake George, where they dragged the boat into the bushes on the shore. Slipping through the woods to within three miles of Ticonderoga, they climbed the mountain that overlooked the fort, which they could see clearly because trees had been cut away around it to make room for tents and huts. They could see the four bastions, a ditch cut out of solid rock at one part, bombproof barracks of stone, and new ramparts of two parallel walls 10 feet apart, built of tree trunks held together by logs with the space between packed with gravel and dirt. From the work parties, the squads drilling, the number of bark canoes on the shore, they could estimate the number of men in the fort. They came down the mountain and neared the fort, hoping to examine it more closely, and happened on three Frenchmen at work. Hoping to take prisoners, the Rangers tried to surround the three, but the French turned and ran to the outer entrenchments. Putnam led the men back up the mountain and along the western ridge, stopping to make a careful survey of every French outpost on Lake George, and then returned to the whaleboat and the fort. General Winslow in his report to Lord Loudon, the commander of the campaign, called this "the best scout yet" and added, "Putnam is a man of strict truth and could be entirely trusted."

In November the French withdrew to the north and the English to the south, the Provincials returned to their homes, and only small holding forces were left to guard the lakes.

Chapter Three

"What Means That Firing Ahead?"

IN JUNE, 1757, Putnam came back to Lake George. He was delighted when his young cousin, Rufus Putnam, 19, tall, redheaded and gangling, arrived with Frye's Massachusetts regiment and was soon released to join the Rangers. In July, six regiments were made from the Provincial force to do scouting duty only, and Putnam was put in command of the two from Connecticut.

Two weeks later, for the first of two times in his life, Putnam disobeyed the orders of a superior officer.

General Lyman had taken over command of Fort Edward, where Putnam was stationed, and he decided to strengthen it still further. One July morning the General sent 150 men to the head of a thick swamp about a half-mile from the fort. They were to cut timber for walls and for an abattis, which was the tops of trees cut with a slanting stroke to make a sharp spike. With the butt end driven in the ground, these made a thick, spiked hedge outside the walls. Fifty regulars went to guard the work

27

party. The swamp was connected with the mainland by a narrow tongue of solid land.

The men had only begun to cut when a sentinel saw several objects fly swiftly from the swamp over his head. He watched them, for he had never seen birds quite like these. He was wondering what they were when one turned into an arrow and buried its head in the tree above him. He fired to give the alarm and dashed toward the others. The work party in the swamp began to retreat. A mass of Indians, who had been hidden among the alders and swamp maples, rushed on the unarmed men and began to tomahawk them, overwhelming the ax-swinging Provincials by sheer numbers. Captain Little and his regulars raced to the swamp, and by hiding in the thick growth and firing on the Indians managed to hold them back a little so some unharmed woodsmen could escape. As they ran past him he called for them to get troops sent from the fort, for he was badly outnumbered.

General Lyman was convinced this was but a beginning of a general attack on the fort and ordered the gates closed. Putnam and his Rangers were camped on an island in the river near the fort. On hearing the firing he hurried from his camp, met the fleeing men, and learned of the danger to the soldiers. Calling to his men to follow, he plunged into the shallow water and began to wade past the walls of the fort.

As he splashed past, holding his musket high, General Lyman climbed on the parapet. "Turn back, Putnam," he shouted. "I will not have more brave men killed to no end. They will be attacking the fort and we will need you here."

Knee-deep in the water, Putnam halted. "Sorry, General," he called back, "but I can't let my good friend Little be slaughtered out there." He waded on, his men following.

The regulars were still holding their ground at the edge of the solid tongue of land. "Make enough noise to be four times your number, boys," Putnam told his men as they caught up with him. With a stentorian shout he led them down the strip of hard ground and into the swamp. Shouting and making enough noise for six times their number, the Rangers crashed after him, firing, loading, whooping, and firing again. The Indians surrounding the regulars thought the whole army was on them. They broke and fled into the woods. The Rangers pursued them until dark. Only one of Putnam's men was killed, and he was quickly avenged.

During the last week in July, General Webb, who was now in command of the army and the two forts, left Fort Edward for Lake George. He took Putnam and 200 men as his guard. At Fort William Henry it was learned that some Rangers had failed to discover any sign of the enemy on a scout the previous night, in spite of earlier word the French were on the move. Putnam begged for permission to make a daylight scout and at last was allowed to leave with 18 volunteers in three whaleboats. At Northwest Bay they spied soldiers on an island. One boat was sent back to report, while the other two bobbed on the blue water with lines and nets out as though fishing. General Webb sent up a skiff to bring Putnam back for a personal report, and when he had heard it, ordered him to stay in the fort. Putnam protested so vehemently against leaving his men to be captured that at last he was allowed to return to the two boats; since Webb had forgotten to order him to come back immediately, the three boats moved farther north until, with the help of his telescope, he saw far away a flotilla sweeping down the lake. Fishing lines were pulled in, oars put out, and boats turned. The French vanguard saw them, and canoes sped to capture the fishermen and only halted the chase two miles from the fort.

Putnam reported that an army was coming to attack. "You will say nothing of this," ordered General Webb sternly. "We will return to Fort Edward tomorrow."

"I hope your Excellency does not intend to neglect so fair an opportunity of giving battle should the enemy presume to land here," protested Putnam.

"What good do you think we should do here?" asked the General curtly. "Prepare the guard to leave at noon."

The French were indeed coming to attack Fort William Henry. An army of 8,000 under the Marquis de Montcalm, one of the ablest and greatest men Old France sent to New France, surrounded the fort the first week in August and started a formal siege. The English had 2,500 men divided between the fort itself and an armed camp nearby. Colonel Monro, a brave Scotsman, left in a command at the fort, sent appeal after appeal for help to General Webb, a coward and a bad general. Webb, afraid of a possible attack on Fort Edward, refused to send any of his own troops or to allow Putnam to take his Rangers or Sir William Johnson to take his men and Indians to the aid of the besieged fort. Monro held out for eight days, until only 300 effective men were left in the fort, and then surrendered.

The French Indians burst into the fort and tomahawked and scalped the wounded and sick. Then, as the

30

unarmed soldiers, women, and children, with French promises of safety, marched from the gates, there came a war whoop from the Abenaki Christians (French Indian allies), and the savages began slaughtering the advancing people. Led by Montcalm, the French officers tried to stop the massacre, which inflamed the Indians further. The Canadian officers, when beseeched for help, merely shrugged and advised everyone to run into the woods. The next morning the Indians sailed north with 700 to 800 prisoners. The French soldiers stayed a week to destroy the fort. Many of the prisoners were later redeemed by Montcalm, and other officers and Canadians, but many were lost forever to their families. Putnam and his Rangers were the first sent by Webb to the fort. There they found the smouldering ruins and the robbed and mutilated corpses of men, women, and children.

Whether he was right or wrong to hold his troops in reserve, General Webb's refusal to go to the aid of the Fort disgusted both the colonies and England, and caused him to be removed from his command. The massacre at Fort William Henry increased still further the hatred of the New Englanders for the French and Canadians and made them more determined than ever to wipe out the enemy to the north.

Again Putnam spent the winter in and near Fort Edward, where Colonel Haviland was now the commandant. The Rangers camped on a nearby island in the Hudson River. One night in midwinter, the barracks inside the fort took fire. These barracks ended just 12 feet from the magazine where 300 barrels of gunpowder were stored. The fire spread quickly. Haviland fired some cannon shot at the supports of the upper floor to try to bring down the second story and keep the fire from being spread by the wind, but without effect.

Putnam, seeing the fire from his island, crossed on the ice and arrived with his Rangers. After one glance at the barracks and the magazine, he ordered the longest ladder to be set against the wall of the magazine, organized his men into a fast, tight bucket brigade, mounted the ladder, and began throwing water over the smouldering roof and walls that held the powder. Someone had thrust a pair of blanket mittens on his hands. When these caught fire and burned, he threw them away.

"Come down," shouted Colonel Haviland from below. "There is nothing you can do. I am emptying the fort."

"Beg permission to stay, sir," Putnam shouted back. "If we do not save the magazine we will all be destroyed." Another pair of mittens was passed up to him as a rafter fell and a torrent of sparks rushed upward into the blackness.

"If you can stay we can," called the Colonel. "Here, men, get more buckets. Nothing more is to be carried out of the fort. Hurry. If we must be blown up we will all go together."

The barracks collapsed with a crash and a roar and an eruption of sparks and flaming bits of wood. Long arms of flames reached for the magazine.

Putnam dropped down the ladder, seized another bucket, and dashed it against the steaming wooden wall. Half smothered in a cloud of cinders, he stood between the burning barracks and the smouldering wall of the magazine, hurling bucket after bucket of icy water. His clothes were scorched, his skin blistered, but an hour later

32

the fire in the barracks had died away. Just one thickness of charred wood still protected the powder barrels. When the mittens were pulled from his hands the skin came with them, and it was a month before he recovered from his burns. Haviland could not praise him enough for saving the fort and the garrison.

That fall Lord Abercrombie had been put in charge of the English forces in the colonies. Putnam was made a major by the Connecticut Assembly, which also voted to raise 5,000 men for the campaign the next spring. This was to be a three-pronged effort: one attack under Major General Jeffrey Amherst would be against the fortress of Louisbourg on the Atlantic coast; one under General John Forbes would attack Fort Duquesne in western Pennsylvania; one under Abercrombie himself would move against Ticonderoga and Crown Point. By the last week in June, 6,000 regular troops and 9,000 Provincials were at Lake George, where Abercrombie formally proclaimed that the capitulation terms of the surrender the previous year were null and void because the enemy had broken them by murdering and capturing the surrendered garrison.

With Abercrombie, as his second in command, thirty-four-year-old Brigadier General George Augustus, Viscount Howe, had come from England. General Wolfe said he was "the noblest Englishman that has appeared in my time and the best soldier in the British army," and Pitt, the Prime Minister, called him "a complete model of military virtue." The army at Lake George, from sutler to general, knew, trusted, and loved him. During the winter and spring months he had joined the Rangers, sometimes with Putnam, sometimes with Rogers, in their scouting parties so as to learn woods warfare at first hand. He had then ordered soldiers and officers of the British army to cut their hair close, wear leggings against briars, cut down the loads they carried, and brown the barrels of their muskets; he set them an example by washing his own shirts. Ordinarily the supercilious British officers looked down on the Provincial officers and men and showed their disdain and scorn, which all the Provincials, and particularly those from New England, who knew they were as good as anyone, resented bitterly and deeply. Howe, by making good friends of many of the Provincial officers, had helped to break down, temporarily, the barriers between the colonials and the regulars. He was such a brave, gay, intelligent, and accomplished young man that Mrs. Schuyler, wife of the great Albany landowner, Major Philip Schuyler, with whom he had stayed at Saratoga, embraced him with tears when he left to march northward.

On the fifth of July an army of 15,000 men in 900 bateaux and 135 whaleboats, with additional flatboats to carry the artillery, started down Lake George. The sun shone on sparkling blue waters, on flashing oars, on the glitter of gold on braid and buttons and gleaming gun barrels. The uniform-filled boats, red in the center for the regulars, blue on the flanks for the Provincials, with the tan of the Rangers in van and rear guard, moved in a stately column three miles wide. The flags of the corps waved proudly in the breeze; bugles, trumpets, or bagpipes played, or drums beat the rhythm for the rowers; all in the vast host were in high spirits. At five in the evening the flotilla reached Sabbath Day Point, 25 miles down the lake, where the army waited until ten for the baggage before moving on. At daybreak they had entered the second narrows, and an advance party of Rangers under Rogers and Putnam, and accompanied by Lord Howe, went ahead in whaleboats to reconnoiter for a landing place.

Some French were found on shore but were easily driven away. By noon the army had landed, formed into four columns, and begun to advance. But the huge trees grew so thickly, and the underbrush was so dense, that it was impossible to see more than a few yards in any direction. Fallen trees, criss-crossed haphazardly as they had fallen, were a further danger. The columns broke formation because of the difficulty of marching, and each man struggled forward as best he could in the heavy heat and deep shade. The guides became bewildered. The army lost all sense of direction. An advance party of French, about 300, who had been watching the English, tried to retreat through the forest, and they also became lost in the bewildering maze of trees.

Lord Howe, Putnam, and 200 of his Rangers were at the head of the first column. Suddenly from the bushes on their left came the French challenge, "Qui vive?" "Français," came the answer, but the French knew better. They fired. The English answered.

"Putnam," said Lord Howe, "what means that firing ahead?"

"I know not, but with your Lordship's leave will see," Putnam replied.

"I will accompany you," said Howe.

"My Lord, if I am killed the loss of my life will be of little consequence, but the preservation of yours is of infinite importance to this army."

"Putnam, your life is as dear to you as mine is to me. I am determined to go."

With a hundred Rangers, Putnam and Lord Howe filed toward the firing. They came upon the French. Both sides fired. Lord Howe was killed instantly. The shooting grew general, and all was confusion. The Rangers farther ahead turned and caught the French between two fires; only about 50 escaped.

Because of the underbrush and failure of the guides, the columns became more and more confused and bewildered. On the left wing the advance glimpsed some of Putnam's men moving ahead over the dead bodies of the slain, thought them French, and began a brisk fire. Putnam's men halted, scattered, and tried to show by signs they were friends. Uncomprehending, and fearing an ambush, the others continued firing. At length, when several Rangers had been killed, Putnam leaped from behind a tree and ran through the bushes and the stream of bullets to the head of the advance. Only then did they stop shooting their comrades.

But the loss to the English in the death of Lord Howe was fatal and irreparable. He had been the heart and soul and brain of the army. It produced, said Robert Rogers, "a consternation through the whole army." "In Lord Howe, the soul of General Abercrombie's army seemed to expire," wrote Major Mante, who was also there. "The death of one man," said the great historian Parkman, "was the ruin of fifteen thousand." But, more than that, Howe was one of those men whose death perhaps changed the course of history of two nations, for he understood both the colonials and his own people, and he might have softened or even averted the conflicts that were to develop.

From the moment of his death, the expedition was mismanaged. The army was kept in arms all night, returned wearily to the landing place, and then advanced again.

Fort Ticonderoga stood on a rocky promontory at the head of Lake Champlain. The forest had been cut down on the sloping ground and the trees left lying among the stumps, tops pointing outward. In front of the trench, outside the walls, an immense abattis had been constructed of great branches criss-crossed and interwoven, with sharpened points bristling like a porcupine. All could be swept by cross-fire from the fort, whose walls were so high only the soldiers' hats could be seen. Abercrombie sent a young and totally inexperienced engineer to survey the defenses from a hill a mile away. Not understanding what he saw, the officer reported the fort could be taken by a bayonet charge. Abercrombie asked for no further survey or confirmation. He had a number of alternatives for reducing the fort; the easiest and simplest would have been to bring up his artillery and knock down the log walls. He chose the worst course and ordered the British to charge, cross the abattis and trenches, and storm the walls.

For four hours, with stubborn, desperate courage, the British regulars charged, withdrew, re-formed, and charged again. They could not penetrate or clamber over the bristling fire-swept mass of trees, where red coats soon hung amid dying leaves. At word of each repulse, Abercrombie, a mile and a half away, who had not come near enough to the fort to see it, ordered another charge. Again the columns would doggedly advance, to turn into a mass of shouting, cursing, screaming men, caught in the branches, swept by cross-fire, struggling to reach a foe they could not see. Even the gallant and famous 42nd, the Black Watch, on the sixth charge, could not reach the walls. Putnam was with the Provincials as they also attacked on the flanks and also were forced to retreat. At twilight Abercrombie at last gave orders to withdraw. He had lost nearly 2,000 men. The French, under the direction of Montcalm, had not lost 500. That very night the British began their retreat, first to the landing place, and then up the lake.

Abercrombie moved the most swiftly of all, though the army arrived at Fort William Henry before sunset. Terrified lest Montcalm follow and attack, Abercrombie hurried on to Fort Edward, leaving the army with orders to strengthen the fort. English and Provincials alike were so disgusted at his abandoning the attack on Ticonderoga so precipitately, at the ignorance and stupidity of his orders, and at his cowardice, that they referred to him as "Mrs. Nabbercromby" (from the scornful adjective namby-pamby) in their letters home telling of their defeat and disgrace. The colonial resentment against the British for the bungling and failure of the campaign grew even stronger.

Chapter Four

The Roads to Montreal

ALTHOUGH BAD FOOD and disease and the scattering of troops weakened the British army, Montcalm, at Ticonderoga, was content to strengthen the fort and send out frequent war parties by way of Wood Creek and South Bay to harass the British and break the lines of communication and supply between their two forts. The Rangers, in turn, were constantly in the forests, endeavoring to discover the raids in time to warn the forts.

One afternoon Putnam and five of his Rangers were lying in a flat-bottomed bateau under some bushes on the east side of the Hudson waiting for some sign or sound of raiders. On the river below them foamed a long series of dangerous rapids. There had been no sign of Indians, and they were about to pull upstream and return to the fort when Putnam noticed two men on the west shore of the river waving to him and pointing back. Then they made gestures of scalping and shooting and pointed to a small tree. Putnam realized they were telling him that a

39

band of Indians as numerous as the leaves on a tree was behind him. One of the Rangers had strayed away from the river. Putnam gave a turkey call and waited. The two men on the opposite shore began to run. It would imperil the whole party to wait longer, so the bateau was pushed out into the river. Upstream on the east bank appeared some dark figures. The river was too fast and deep for them to swim to the bateau, and if Putnam tried to cross to the opposite shore they would all be shot like ducks, for the river was not very wide. The rapids and falls downstream meant almost certain death by drowning, but at least it was a chance. The missing Ranger did not return. A call and a shout came from the running Indians.

"Row out," ordered Putnam. A bullet landed on the side of the bateau. The next two splashed in the water. The current seized the heavy boat and began to push it ahead.

"Sit on the bottom," Putnam told the four men as he moved sedately to the stern seat and seized the steering oar.

Spray ahead showed the first rock ledges with their tumbling water. On the shore the Indians halted to watch and then began to run along the bank. The men in the boat straightened, took one look at the rapids, whitened, and crouched down again.

"Don't worry, lads. We'll make it," Putnam told them cheerfully. Serenely he moved the steering sweep and the bateau tipped and rounded a wide rock, dipped down a smooth rapid, was caught in an eddy, swirled and was steered around another ledge, caught and turned bow to stern, and thrust backwards as spray dashed across the men. A rush of water lifted the bow, then plunged it down to another pool and out a narrow passage between shelving rocks. The men watched Putnam and then the river with terror, admiration, and wonder.

On the bank the Indians stopped. Careening, dipping, rising, tossed from side to side, mounting a crest of a wave above a rapids, then turned sideways in an eddy and plunging down around a rock and through a passage between ledges, the bateau sped down the rapids to the smooth water a quarter of a mile below. The Indians were so impressed by the skill of the man who had steered the boat they agreed he was invulnerable, a favorite of the Great Spirit, and one who should not be attacked. They returned north without attempting any raid.

But once Putnam's courage and skills were overwhelmed.

In August a large party of French and Indians surprised and destroyed a wagon train of provisions coming from Fort Edward. Abercrombie ordered Rogers, with Provincials under Putnam, some Rangers and Light Infantry, to go down Lake George in boats to try to cut off the marauders at the narrows. The French, however, escaped. On the way back orders arrived to intercept other parties said to be around Fort Edward. After scouting in separate parties, marching in silence and without fires at night, they came together and camped on the lower end of Wood Creek. There had been no signs of the enemy. The morning of August 8th, Rogers forgot his usual caution, and because of an argument with a lieutenant of the light infantry, set up a mark in a clearing and they began to fire at it on a wager. Putnam's protests were ignored. The famous French partisan and Indian leader, Marin, with a band of 400, was a mile and a half away. The sound of the shots came to him sharply.

The clearing where the British had camped was an open space in a tight second growth of saplings and bushes. The only way through it was a narrow Indian path. The morning dew glittered in the sunlight as, in single file, the British started north. Putnam marched at the head of the column, followed by his Provincials; the Light Infantry under Captain Dalzell came next, with Rogers and his men in the rear.

As Putnam stepped out of the thick growth into the forest beyond, Marin sprang his ambush. From a semi-circle around the path his men poured fire on the Provincials. Putnam shouted to halt, take cover, and for a runner to go back to warn the other troops. Then he ran to the nearest bush and began to load and fire. But from a thicket on the right a whooping Caughnawaga, hatchet uplifted, sprang at him. Putnam thrust his musket against the painted chest and pulled the trigger. The gun missed fire. The Indian shouted and grappled with him. Two others jumped on him from behind, and he was dragged by the three into the edge of the forest. His feet were tied together, his arms jerked behind his back and around a small tree and tied. With another whoop the warriors sprang away toward the battle.

So thick was the brush that it was a half-hour before the Light Infantry and Rangers could come up to the enemy. Then the action shifted back and forth, as each man fought on his own. At first the British gave ground and the Indians pursued them, then the British gathered, turned, and drove back the French forces. This change brought the tree where Putnam was tied between the two fields of fire. Leaves clipped from their stems by bullets and arrows drifted down around him. For an hour, shots were fired on all sides: bullets whined overhead; bullets struck the tree and three went through his jacket; arrows fled past his head. A young warrior, shifting from tree to tree, suddenly noticed the bound man. With a joyous shriek he hurled the tomahawk at the tree above Putnam's head, pulled it out and hurled it again, laughing heartily as the prisoner tried to dodge and bend. Another warrior, watching, doubled up with mirth. Tiring of the game, the two slid off to fight some more.

A French petty officer, changing ground, noticed the prisoner, raised his gun, and fired point-blank at Putnam's chest. The musket missed fire.

"Prisoner of war. Don't shoot. Prisoner of war," protested Putnam.

The Frenchman seized the muzzle of his gun and swung the butt against Putnam's ribs. As Putnam protested again, the man swung the butt at his face. It struck Putnam's jaw and left a scar he carried the rest of his life. The man started to swing again, heard a shout, and hurried away.

Putnam stopped struggling against his bonds and listened. The sounds of battle moved south as the British retreated, then came north again. If the French had to retreat quickly, perhaps the Indians would forget him. But the tall warrior who had captured him leaped beside the tree, untied the knots, and leading him by a rawhide thong, dashed into the forest. Putnam could see the French and Indians flitting north between the trees.

Once the warrior looked back at his prisoner. "Me, Master," he said cheerfully. Putnam nodded as he tried to keep up the pace.

A call from ahead made the warrior thrust the end of

43

the thong into the hands of another Indian before he loped away. The new Indian halted, untied Putnam, and gestured for him to take off his clothes. Surrounded now by a grinning circle, Putnam took off coat, vest, stockings, and, reluctantly, shoes. His arms were tied tightly above the elbow to his sides, his wrists bound closely together, and three packs were piled and tied on his shoulders. Slipping, stumbling, the wound on his left cheek bleeding, he followed his captors.

He fell when they halted. His hands were swollen from the cords and the pain was intolerable; his feet were bleeding; he had no breath or strength left. But when he saw a pair of boots among the brown legs around him he managed to roll over. A white man was looking at him curiously.

"You an officer?" Putnam croaked.

"No. I'm just the interpreter."

"For God's sake then ask these savages to knock me on the head and take my scalp and be done with it. Or at least loosen my hands."

"Hunh. You *are* in a bad way. These wild men won't do anything for me, but I'll look for an officer. Though they probably won't obey anything he tells them to do."

Putnam closed his eyes and waited.

There was a sound of Indian gabbling around him. Another pair of boots stood amid the moccasins. The packs were being untied and the thongs about his arms and hands removed. He could not help groaning as the blood flowed into his hands. He managed to sit up. A French officer, his white trousers dirty and his blue coat torn, was gesticulating to a row of stolid painted faces. A taller figure loomed behind them.

44

"Master," groaned Putnam as loudly as he could.

The Caughnawaga warrior shoved through the group and looked at Putnam. He began to harangue the other Indians fiercely, pointing to his prisoner's feet and face and shaking his fist around the circle. He stopped shouting, pulled a pair of moccasins from one of the packs and tied them on Putnam's feet and pulled him upright. The French officer watched. The chief said something to the interpreter, who jerked his thumb towards the sullen Indians.

"They're going ahead to find a camp for the night," he told Putnam. "They're taking you with them. Your man —he's a chief in case you didn't recognize the marks, and you better call him master every other word since it pleases them and won't do you any harm—has to go back to care for the wounded. He'll come up with you later."

The red and black stripes on the Caughnawaga's face stretched in a smile. He patted Putnam on the head, saw only one pack was put on his shoulders and that his hands were tied loosely. Another Indian seized the leading cord.

How many miles or hours they trotted, Putnam never knew. At dusk they halted in a glade in the deep forest. Uneasily he saw there were only Indians in the band. Three of them untied him, pulled off his clothes, pushed him to a sapling in the center of the open space, and tied him to it with green withes. The whole band dropped their weapons and began gathering brush and dead branches, which they piled in a circle about three feet from the sapling. As they gathered and piled they whooped and laughed and pointed and obviously made jokes and bets. When the brush was two feet high, two of them tied his hands behind him around the tree, but

45

loosely, so he could shift his body but not his feet. Sparks struck in tinder at a dozen places set the brush afire. Snatching up their tomahawks, they began to leap and dance around him. The flames took hold, spread. Putnam could feel the heat from a higher blaze on the left and shifted his body. This was a great joke. Some of the warriors shouted and poked the fire. Sudden dark clouds spread above the tree tops, darkened, and a quick shower of rain pelted down and put out the fire. The Indians lay on the ground and waited until it was quite over and the clouds moving away. Then they went off and found some dry tinder from dead trees and rekindled the circle of fire.

This time the fire was stronger on his right, and he twisted away to the left. This was another joke. Putnam knew there was no hope of escaping from the withes that bound him, for they were so green they would not burn; they merely tightened as he struggled..

He also knew there was no hope of rescue by his own men. As the fires blazed he must have thought of his beloved wife and children and his farm, in which he took such pride, and of his soldier friends with whom he would never share again the excitement of battle and the challenging thrill of mortal danger. As the flames rose all around, he stiffened. He could make himself stand still and die properly. One Indian poked a pile of branches closer, and Putnam could feel his skin begin to blister.

From the trees, beyond the circle of light, burst an officer in the uniform of the French partisans. Knocking some Indians aside, he seized a branch and scattered the burning brush, ran through the opening, cut Putnam free, and dragged him beyond the flames. He stood over Put-

46

nam's body and shouted at the Indians. Sullenly, one by one they dropped their tomahawks and began to scatter the burning brush. Reluctantly they returned Putnam's clothes and moccasins.

"I am Marin," the officer said. Putnam knew of him as one of the most famous partisan leaders. "A warrior came to warn me of this. I came to stop it. I will wait with you until your captor arrives."

And wait he did until the Caughnawaga hurried into camp. He, in turn, scolded the Indians, helped Putnam to walk to ease the stiffness. Putnam tried to croak his thanks to Marin, but could hardly make a sound. The officer waved his hand, nodded, and vanished. The Caughnawaga held out some hard biscuits. Putnam shook his head and pointed to the wound on the side of his face to show he could not chew. The Indian nodded, cut some birchbark and made it into a little dish, filled it with water and dipped the biscuits in until they were soft enough for Putnam to suck and swallow.

By now sentinels were being placed, and warriors were dropping off to sleep. The Caughnawaga led Putnam to the edge of a thicket and gestured to him to lie down. Then one arm was extended and tied to a sapling, his moccasins were taken off, each arm and leg was stretched and each hand and foot tied to a tree. To be certain the prisoner did not escape, the Indians then cut down some young trees and trimmed them to poles. These were laid across Putnam's body, on both sides, from neck to foot. As many Indians as could crowd into the space lay down on the ends of the poles and went to sleep. Aching and sleepless, Putnam could not help laughing to himself at the ridiculous picture they all made.

When at dawn the poles were removed and his feet and hands untied, Putnam was so stiff he could not rise. His master had to put on his moccasins and feed him some moistened strips of bear meat. He even threw a blanket around Putnam's shoulders, when he was up, and saw that the leading cord was tied only around his waist. That evening the party arrived at Fort Ticonderoga, and the tattered, scorched, limping Putnam was turned over to the French guard. Some of the Indians showed their anger that he was not given to them to burn now, but his master rubbed his fingers together to show he expected ransom money, and he patted Putnam's head again before he left. The Marquis de Montcalm, a great man and a great general, spoke to the prisoner, ordered him cared for and his wound dressed, and after a short talk through an interpreter sent him on to Montreal. The officer in charge was friendly but not concerned about his prisoner's welfare.

Fortunately for many American prisoners in Montreal, Colonel Peter Schuyler of Albany was also a prisoner on parole. As kind as he was wealthy, Colonel Schuyler had taken it upon himself to help in any way he could the Americans brought into the city. As soon as he heard Putnam had been brought in, he went to call and was horrified to find the major in a small dank cell, without coat or stockings, his clothes filthy, his beard long, his legs and arms torn and blistered, and his face swollen from the untended wound. Schuyler protested so strongly to Governor Vaudreuil that he was allowed to take Putnam to his own house and see he was given proper care.

Exchange was not long in coming. Early in September, Lieutenant Colonel Bradstreet captured Fort Frontenac on Lake Ontario, and now there were French officers to exchange for those held in Montreal. Colonel Schuyler headed the list. The French Governor, grateful because Schuyler had spared him the trouble of looking after so many prisoners, told him he could name any other officer, not already listed, to take back with him to New York. Putnam had not been recognized as the famous Ranger leader, and Schuyler was anxious to get him out of Canada before he should become known. So the Colonel thanked Vaudreuil warmly and said in an offhand fashion, "There is an old man here, a Provincial major, who wishes to go home to join his wife and children. He can do no good here. I believe your Excellency had better keep some of the young men, who have no wife or children to care for, and let the old fellow go home with me."

Vaudreuil agreed he could take the Provincial major and on the list of exchanged prisoners appeared, somehow, the name "Polman, Capt-Maj. in N.E. Regt."

At Schuyler's house there was a widow whose husband had been killed by the Indians and she and her seven children had been taken to Canada. She was also to be returned, and Schuyler put her and her family in Putnam's care, since he had to go ahead and make arrangements for the 150 officers, soldiers, sailors, women, and children who were being exchanged. On the long march from Montreal to Albany, Putnam saw to it that the family had warm food and that their camps at night were properly prepared, and he carried the small children when they were too tired to walk.

He reached his home at last to find he had been made Lieutenant Colonel in the 4th Connecticut regiment.

In 1759, under a new commander, began the last campaign against French Canada.

Major General Jeffrey Amherst was energetic, cautious, experienced, and resolute, a very different commander from Abercrombie. Now in command of another three-pronged attack on Canada, with General James Wolfe to seize Quebec and Colonel Prideaux due to take the fort at Niagara, he himself took over the direction of the central advance against Ticonderoga, Crown Point, and Montreal. An army of 11,000, half Provincials and half regulars, gathered at the head of Lake George in June. They were efficiently organized and drilled, and their well-being was guarded, from the flogging of deserters to discourage the practice, to the daily prayers and sermons twice a week, and the daily draft of spruce beer as a protection against scurvy.

On July 21st another great military pageant of bright uniforms, blue for the Provincials and red for the regulars, with gay flags, martial music, and shining weapons, moved down Lake George. At daylight the next morning the army landed near the outlet, scattered a band of French, and marched to Ticonderoga. The abattis and defense entrenchments, which had foiled the English the previous summer and brought the death of so many gallant men in the six futile charges, were now abandoned, and Amherst's regiments found them fine protection from the guns of the fort. Unlike Abercrombie, Amherst was on the ground to see for himself what the conditions were. He brought up his artillery and prepared to bombard the fort when he found that the French commander, under orders from the Governor, had abandoned it, except for 400 men, and retreated northward to Crown

Point. The captain in charge left a match burning in the powder magazine to blow up the fort and escaped with his men, but only one bastion was blown. So this famous stronghold, that had so long menaced the English provinces and caused so much bloodshed, fell to the British. Crown Point was also abandoned by the French. But the advance on Montreal was delayed by the French fleet on Lake Champlain and the French army at a formidable position on an island in the Richelieu River. It was too late in the season by the time the English fleet was built, so the final reduction of Canada was left for yet another year.

Amherst settled down to build a new and stronger fort at Crown Point that would be a basis for the operations next year. Putnam spent the remainder of the summer and autumn there superintending work parties. In September came word of the capture of Quebec by General Wolfe and his death at the moment of victory, and the death the same day of the gallant Montcalm. Then Fort Niagara was captured by Sir William Johnson. At last the English colonies could confidently foresee the fall of Canada.

That November a son, named Daniel for the son who had died, was born to the Putnam family. Daniel will be met later outside Boston.

In the summer of 1760 came the culmination of five years of British campaigns against the French.

The British army that had wintered at Quebec and then defeated a last French attack was to march westward under General Murray to Montreal. Brigadier Haviland would take the fort at the Isle aux Noix and advance on Montreal from the south. Amherst would lead the main army, gathered at Oswego, down the St. Lawrence River from Lake Ontario to Montreal. This was the longest and most difficult route, but the move was essential to prevent the French forces from retreating to safety in the western wilderness. The three armies were to meet at Montreal at the same time. There was no way they could communicate with each other.

It was May when the troops for the western campaign assembled at Albany and two months later before the 10,000 men had reached the shores of Lake Ontario. In addition to the regulars there were eight battalions of Provincials from New York, New Jersey, and Connecticut under Brigadier General Thomas Gage, an old friend of Putnam's.

On the morning of August 15th, as three divisions in bateaux and whaleboats were nearing the northeast end of Lake Ontario, two French ships were sighted. The English gunboats had become lost among the maze of islands and channels. These two French ships could wreck the soldier-laden bateaux.

While Amherst was pondering what should be done, Putnam came up to him. "General," he said, pointing to the larger ship, "that vessel must be taken."

"Aye," answered the General. "I would give the world if she were."

"I'll take her for you," said Putnam.

Amherst smiled and asked how.

"Give me some wedges, a beetle, a large wood hammer or maul that can be used for driving wedges, and a few men of my own choice."

"How it can be done with such I cannot conceive," said

Amherst, "but take what you need, for those two ships could do us great damage."

That night Putnam put his five men and his tools into a small boat and rowed and drifted down on the French ship so silently the sentinels heard no sound. Slipping to the stern, the men held the rowboat in place while Putnam quickly drove the wedges into the space between the rudder and the hull that gives the rudder free play. As silently as it had come, the boat returned.

In the morning the ship could be seen drifting on the lake, her sails flapping at the masts. The French could not make her respond to the rudder, and a wind drove her ashore. Putnam led a thousand men in 50 bateaux toward the helpless vessel, and as she grounded they boarded her and her flag came down. The other ship was attacked and captured by five gunboats that had found their way at last. The capture of the two ships uncovered Fort Levis on Isle Royale in the middle of the channel of the river. Amherst halted. He wanted no enemy fort left intact in his rear and also he hoped to find in the fort pilots to guide his boats down the rapids and falls of the St. Lawrence.

Again Putnam made an "original and venturesome" suggestion that Amherst approved. Although the fort was surrounded by the English, with guns mounted on two nearby islands, there remained the problem of taking it. A high abattis of black ash projected from the walls of the fort out over the water so far that no ship could approach and land men to storm the walls. Putnam had a number of flat-bottomed boats fitted out with heavy high planks on all sides that were bullet-proof and would protect the men from cannonballs and bullets. Then a wide, heavy plank, 20 feet long, was fitted upright at one end of each boat. This plank was jointed and held upright by ropes so the bows of the boats could be forced against the abattis and the planks could be lowered across it to form gangplanks for the attackers. The garrison surrendered, both because of the bombardment and encirclement and because of the strange sight of the advancing bateaux. The Iroquois of Sir William Johnson were so infuriated that they were not allowed to scalp the prisoners that most of them returned to their villages. The British could now move down the river to Montreal.

The rushing rapids of the St. Lawrence killed more men than had the French defenders; 46 boats were wrecked, and 84 men drowned. But on the morning of September 6th the troops encamped before the walls of Montreal. The tents of Haviland's army were white on the south shore of the river. The next morning Murray's troops arrived and camped to the east. Three armies from three points of the compass had overcome their varying obstacles and arrived practically simultaneously, an amazing military achievement, due in large part to the careful planning of General Amherst. On September 8th Governor Vaudreuil signed the capitulation.

Amherst refused to allow the soldiers and officers to march out of the city with the arms and honors of war because, he said, "I am fully resolved, for the infamous part the troops of France have acted in exciting the savages to perpetrate the most horrid and unheard-of barbarities in the whole progress of the war, and for other open treacheries and flagrant breaches of faith, to manifest to all the world by this capitulation my detestation of such practices."

During the negotiations for the surrender Putnam found at the Christian Indian village of Caughnawaga on the Saut St. Louis the chief who had captured him on the raid two years before. The Indian was delighted to see him, entertained him at his well-built stone house, and hoped Putnam would see that no harm would come to him for fighting against the English. Putnam assured him no harm would come to anyone in Canada and was as pleased as the Indian to find they could be friends.

Canada passed to the British crown. New England rejoiced. There were parades and bonfires, cannon were fired, and sermons gave thanks for the deliverance from the enemy. The northern colonies had learned during the past five years to work together, to raise and support armies, to steadfastly oppose a common enemy. But now there was peace, and Israel Putnam, once more a citizen, returned to his Connecticut farm.

Chapter Five

But There Was No Peace

ALTHOUGH CANADA WAS LOST, the war between France and England continued around the world. In 1761 Charles III of Spain made a treaty, known as "The Family Compact," with Louis XV of France that bound the princes of the House of Bourbon to support each other against the growing power of the King of England. England retaliated by attacking the possessions of both Spain and France in a number of places, including the Caribbean, with the large and wealthy island of Cuba as the ultimate goal. By early June a fleet of 200 vessels, a fifth of them men-of-war, under Admiral Sir George Pocock, and an army of 11,000 under General the Earl of Albermarle, stood off Havana.

Again the colonies had been called on for troops, and again Connecticut had voted to furnish two regiments. Major General Lyman was in command for the eighth year, and Lieutenant Colonel Israel Putnam commanded the first regiment. In May the troops from New England, New York, and New Jersey assembled at New York to take ship for Cuba.

The men were housed for drill and equipment on Nutter's Island, but the officers lived at the taverns in the city. New York City, a mile long and half a mile wide, because of its trade was the most prosperous city of the colonies. Though it had been in English hands for many years, the Dutch language was still spoken by many of the people. The narrow streets, thronged with handsome, bustling crowds, were paved with large round pebbles and lined with well-built brick houses, many with stepped gables from Dutch days. Broadway and the Bowery, wide and tree-lined, with shops and large private homes with gardens, were the most important thoroughfares. The 14-foot stockade with blockhouses and gates still stood across the island, though the Indian threat had long vanished. The only water held fit to make tea came from the "tea-water" pump, always surrounded by housewives and servants carrying pitchers. The shores were lined with wharves, warehouses, and ships, from men-of-war to scows used to ferry people and produce east to the village of Brooklyn or west across the Hudson River to Paulus Hook in New Jersey. North of the city were abrupt little hills, stretches of woods, ponds and many brooks, little villages, small farms, and the imposing country estates, with orchards, gardens, and pastures, of the wealthy merchants.

New York was gay as well as prosperous. At the Fort, a gray massive quadrangle south of Bowling Green that held the Governor's palace and the barracks, there was a great deal of military entertaining. In addition to private parties, there were dinners at the many taverns—the

Bull's Head, The King's Arms, The Queen's Head, A Dish of Fry'd Oysters—and often gaming. Always available were marionette shows, waxworks, amusement gardens, bull or bear baiting, and shooting matches beyond the walls. One of the most popular pastimes was horse racing on the various tracks beyond Bowery Village, where ladies drove in their carriages and officers and citizens met to race and bet. Even though there were occasional duties with their troops, the Provincial officers found New York a fascinating and delightful place.

On June 10th the assembled troops boarded 18 ships and started southward along the white and green shores of New Jersey, only to run aground off Sandy Hook. It was backbreaking work to unload, lighten, and load the ships again. Putnam's Provincials, along with an added Rhode Island company, were crowded so tightly into one ship that each soldier was allowed just five feet by two of space, and the officers fared little better. When well at sea, Putnam spoke from the poop to the crowded deck. He told them where they were going, and why, and that he was assured the war would be short and there would be good pay at the end. The men were to drill on deck twice a day, but must spend the rest of the time between decks and lie on their gear at night.

As the ships pushed south the air grew warmer. Putnam shared the two meals a day with the men. With them he learned to knock the iron-hard ship's biscuits on the floor so the weevils would crawl out, and then to drop the biscuits in the watery soup so they could be chewed, to swallow boiled rice that was musty and covered with dead moths, to relish the one small piece of meat every four days, and to drink the fresh water that soon carried a green scum. He allowed no complaining—these were just hardships, minor ones, that were different from those encountered campaigning on land.

Then, one afternoon, far to the south rose a narrow line of blue darker than the blue water—Cuba. With the white sails of the other transports dipping to right and left, the ship plowed on beneath suddenly mounting thunder heads of clouds and darkening skies. At midnight the storm broke. Thunder crashed, lightning ran up and down the rigging, and a fierce wind and gigantic waves drove the pitching ship. All the troops were ordered on deck. There they waited, packed in ranks so tightly even the pitching and rolling of the ship could not displace a man. When the lightning flared, their eyes were on the stalwart figure of Putnam holding fast to the rail of the poop. There came a pause in the shrieking wind long enough for the men to hear the lookout cry "Breakers ahead."

"Dress ranks," shouted Putnam in a mighty voice that carried through wind and rain. "We're going to hit."

From beneath the bow came a grinding crash. A wave lifted the ship and set it down with a second crash. The ship halted, tilted, and the men were tipped toward the stern. With each wave the ship settled a little lower.

"At ease," Putnam shouted. "We'll man the pumps by squads. No man is to move except on orders." No man did.

Dawn showed the reef beneath the ship was a long one, and that many other ships were also aground. Every man who could wield a saw or hammer was put to making rafts from spars and planks to supplement the ship's boats. By sunrise the first were ready to be towed by the sailors rowing the dories. Under Putnam's watchful eyes the fully equipped men climbed down the slanting side to sit in stiff rows on the bobbing rafts. Brown cliffs and a green forest beyond were not a mile away. By afternoon every soldier had been landed and not a man had been lost. The storm had driven the transports too far to the east of Havana. Two days later the Provincials were moved to the west of the city, at Chorrera, where the English grenadiers and also the other troops from the colonies were camped. The siege of the city had been going on for two months but there had been little fighting. Since nearly half of the English troops were sick from spoiled food, bad water, and the heat, the fresh soldiers from the north were very welcome. But soon the Provincials came down with the fevers also.

Morro Castle, high on a cliff at the entrance to the spacious harbor, was the key to Havana. In July British engineers brought down, by blasting with gunpowder, a portion of the cliff to the west, and the fall of rock made a narrow bridge across the great moat. Twenty men, led by a young officer, crossed the rocks and climbed into the fort, and the fort surrendered. Ten days later, after one day of bombardment, the Spanish surrendered Havana. The Provincials who were strong enough were put to work to make repairs on the walls and fortifications.

One afternoon when Putnam was walking near the harbor he came on an angry Spaniard beating a slave with a bamboo cane. Although he was alone and unarmed, Putnam rushed to the Spaniard, tore the cane from his hand, and began to beat him. The street had been empty, but in a moment the three were surrounded by a mob of Cubans and Spaniards furious at the behavior of the foreigner. Putnam broke and ran for the nearest English ship, and safety, the slave, Dick, at his heels. On board the ship, the Negro begged to be saved from a cruel master and allowed to become Putnam's servant. Both cane and Dick returned to Pomfret with him in October when the Provincial troops that survived (400 in Putnam's own command died) were sent back to the colonies.

When the final treaty was made at Paris between France, England and Spain, France surrendered Canada and lands east of the Mississippi to England, and New Orleans and Louisiana to Spain. Cuba was returned to Spain in exchange for the Floridas.

But though there was now peace between the great powers, there was no peace on the western borders of the colonies. The Indians of the western lands beyond Pennsylvania, Chippewas, Hurons, Ottawas, Delawares, Shawnees, Wyandots, were driven to fury and despair by France's giving away their lands to the English. Then General Amherst cut off the multitude of gifts with which the British had formerly tried to hold the allegiance of the tribes, because he believed the evidence of British power would impress the savages sufficiently to keep them friendly. But the Indians united against the white invaders, who settled on the land instead of merely hunting for skins for export as had the French. Forts from Michigan to Pennsylvania were captured, soldiers and settlers killed, and the British army was unable to protect the frontier cabins or punish the tribes. Detroit itself was under siege by the Ottawas, led by their chief Pontiac, who had started and encouraged the uprising, until at last, after six months, a truce was agreed upon. General Amherst returned to England in October, 1763, and General Thomas Gage was left to crush the Indian uprising. He planned a pincer movement, one force under Colonel Bouquet to enter Ohio by way of Fort Pitt, in western Pennsylvania, and another under Colonel Bradstreet to go by boat from Niagara to Detroit and then move southward. Again troops were raised from the colonies and again Colonel Israel Putnam was in command of the regiment from Connecticut.

At Albany in June, 1764, Putnam found two old friends. One was Lieutenant (and engineer) John Montresor, who had been with his father, a Major, in the British forces under Amherst. The other was the Caughnawaga chieftain who had come with a hundred of his own tribe to join the warriors of the Six Nations under Sir William Johnson. After a month spent in conferences and the smoking of pipes with chiefs from some of the enemy tribes and in building a fort at the mouth of Lake Erie, designed by Montresor and supervised by Putnam, the army set out on Lake Erie. A few days later, Bradstreet, though his orders from Gage were to chastize and subdue the hostile tribes, stopped the voyage to give easy peace terms to three tribes. He agreed to meet all at Sandusky in 25 days to receive the white captives they would release and to ratify the treaty. The army then moved on to Detroit, but because of high winds and waves the voyage took two weeks.

Fort Detroit stood at the western end of Lake Erie on the western bank of the mouth of the River Raisin. A palisade wall about 25 feet high, with bastions at each corner and a blockhouse at each gateway, surrounded about a hundred houses. Bradstreet and his army were welcomed with a cannon salute and salvos from the friendly Indians. Another old friend of Putnam's, from the Lake George expeditions, was the commander, Major Gladwyn. He knew and understood the Indian mentality and emotions, as did Putnam, but Bradstreet would listen to no advice. He held another futile council and only moved south sluggishly when Gage sent him a furious letter.

Putnam admired northern Ohio. He wrote to a friend that there were many places of ten or twenty thousand acres without a bush or twig, covered with grass so high traveling was difficult, but all on the best land he had ever seen. He told of the beauties of the lake and land around Detroit and of Bradstreet's stupid treatment of the Indian chiefs. That Colonel decided it was too far to go to meet Colonel Bouquet on the Scioto River, as planned, so he made some meaningless treaties and returned to Niagara, losing troops and ships in storms on the way. Not a blow had been struck against the hostile tribes. At Niagara the army was disbanded, and Putnam reached home early in December. This time he was not to take up arms again for 11 years.

The Colonel Israel Putnam who returned to Pomfret was very different from the Private Putnam who had gone out to fight the French and Indians ten years before. Few men were now more famous. Few New Englanders of the same rank had seen such varied military service with His Majesty's forces and none had played a more honorable part in each of the military campaigns. And Putnam, quite conscious that his schooling had been stopped too early, had undoubtedly watched and listened and learned from men of experience and education, such as Lord Howe, Amherst, Gage, Gladwyn, Montresor, with whom he had passed so many months. They had liked and admired him for his courage, good cheer, and kindness, and he had always been welcome at their table and campfire. Wherever he went he made friends in all ranks—and kept them. His fellow citizens and the people of New England respected him for his bravery, patriotism, and integrity.

It was the duty of a patriot to serve his country, but it was also his duty to resist tyranny. To the colonists in 1765 the imposition of the Stamp Act by England was tyranny. This was a tax to pay for the costs of the conquest of Canada and meant that a stamp costing a few pennies must be bought and affixed to all documents such as bills of sale or wills. But this tax was imposed on the American colonies by a Parliament in which they were not represented and which allowed them no voice in how the money was collected or spent. In addition to the injustice, the successful imposition of the tax would establish a precedent for more and heavier taxes in the future. From Samuel Adams in Boston to Patrick Henry in Virginia there were outbursts of fury, speeches, resolutions, and meetings on how best to defeat the tax.

Putnam and two other gentlemen were named by a meeting of citizens to call on Governor Fitch at Hartford and warn him against seeing that the stamps were used and the tax collected. After some talk of this and that, Governor Fitch asked, "What should I do if the stamped paper is sent to me by the King's authority?"

"Lock it up until we visit you again," Putnam told him.

"And what will you do then?"

"We shall expect you to give us the key of the room in which the paper is deposited, and, if you think fit, in order to screen yourself from blame, you may forewarn us, upon our peril, not to enter the room."

"And what will you do afterwards?"

"Send the stamps back again."

"But if I should refuse admission to the room?"

"In such a case, your house will be leveled with the dust in five minutes."

It was believed that one of the reasons why stamped paper was never sent into Connecticut was the report of this conversation by the royal governor. Because of the fierce resistance of the colonists, the Stamp Act was repealed by Parliament a year later. When the news came, Connecticut held a day of public thanksgiving, with church services, illuminations, and bonfires. This resistance to the Stamp Act gave great impetus to the growth of secret societies in the colonies against what they felt was the tyranny of England. The most famous was the Sons of Liberty, with chapters in most of the towns, who exchanged information and advice. Putnam was an important and inspiring member of his chapter and he rode often from town to town to find out which men could be trusted and where arms and ammunition could be safely stored. The constant activity among the chapters helped pave the way for the cooperation among the colonies in later years.

In an accident on his farm, Putnam lost the first joint of his right thumb, and later he broke his right thigh so badly that his right leg became an inch shorter than the other, so he always walked with a limp. For two years he represented Pomfret in the Colonial Legislature at Hartford.

In 1766 his wife, Hannah, died. For 26 years she had raised her family and helped her husband make the farm prosperous and managed it while he was with the Provincial troops. She left seven children, the youngest, Peter Schuyler Putnam, just three months old.

In June of 1767 he married Mrs. Deborah Lothrop Gardiner. They had known each other when she was the wife of a minister in the nearby village of Brooklyn. At the death of her husband she had married John Gardiner 5th, the proprietor of Gardiner's Island, an estate, held by that family for nearly two hundred years, off the eastern tip of Long Island. The new Mrs. Putnam knew many of the prominent families on both sides of the Sound and was accustomed to entertaining. Putnam was now the most prominent man in eastern Connecticut and the champion of the patriot cause against English tyranny. Both he and his wife were friendly and hospitable, and their home was constantly filled with visitors. Passing soldiers called on the famous and beloved Colonel: patriots came to take new fire from his pungent and pithy discussion of politics: distinguished strangers journeying between Hartford and Providence stopped to meet the hero. The cost of feeding the horde became too great for even a successful farmer. Some way had to be found to save himself from ruin. Since his oldest son, Israel, was now married, Putnam turned the home farm over to him. Next he moved the rest of his family to a substantial house owned by Mrs. Putnam on the green in Brooklyn.

This large and comfortable house was then turned into "The General Wolfe" tavern. The signboard had Wolfe, the conqueror of Quebec, in his long red coat and white breeches, high boots and tricorn hat, pointing with his right hand while some soldiers appeared vaguely in the background. Soon inn and signboard were well known throughout New England. The village tavern was, next to the town hall, the most important building in the village, for here were posted not only notices of town meetings, of new laws, and of local sales, but news of the outside world was brought here. Coaches stopped to rest or change horses, and passengers and travelers would put up for the night. Each night there was a gathering around the wide hearth. Putnam was always, anywhere, a good companion, and enjoyed whatever he was doing. Just as he had always been eager in his Ranger days for any adventure or excitement, now he enjoyed good talk, good company, good food, and any activity from a dance to a house-raising. He never picked a quarrel, but upheld his opinions with vigor, good nature, and common sense. His devotion to liberty was so deep and strong he could inspire all who came within his orbit. His fairness and integrity were so trusted by his fellow townsmen that he moderated at town meetings, superintended the building of bridges and roads, engaged schoolmasters, oversaw the collection of taxes, and was chosen to count and pay for crows' heads when a bounty of sixpence was offered on each head. He tolled the church bell, which only prominent citizens were permitted to do, for a payment of three pounds a year.

He was always ready to help, as far as he could, anyone poor or in trouble. The Provincial soldiers who were veterans of the French and Indian wars had been promised grants of land as a part of their pay when the wars were over. General Lyman spent ten years in England trying to obtain the necessary papers. In 1772 he returned to Connecticut, convinced the papers would be sent immediately. A "Company of Military Adventurers" was formed to see the plans carried out, and a committee, with Putnam at its head, was sent to explore the proposed grants on the Mississippi. At Pensacola Putnam found two old friends, Major John Small and Colonel Frederick Haldimand, but no papers. Lyman had been so sure all was well that the committee went on to New Orleans and up the Mississippi to the Yazoo, only to find the lands were held by the Choctaw tribe and so covered with impenetrable canebrake that the quality of the soil could not be judged. They returned to Pensacola to learn that the Governor of West Florida had not received the papers from England (they never did arrive), and then went back to Connecticut with their discouraging report. Nothing further could be done because of the inertia and lack of interest shown by the British government. The Company disbanded, and the veterans never received their promised lands.

Chapter Six

"Justice Would Be on Our Side"

BUT EVEN MORE IMPORTANT MATTERS than the plight of
veterans were crowding insistently into the life of Israel
Putnam. The stubborn British government thought of
the colonists as Englishmen living at a distance and never
realized that the new lands were making a new kind of
men. The colonists were equally stubborn and determined
to defend the liberties and measure of independence England had granted them in the colonial charters.

In London, the House of Commons had for ten years
been determined to make the colonies help pay the bill for
the Seven Years' War and the defeat of the French and
Spanish around the world. The colonies felt they had
done their share. First England imposed the Sugar Act,
taxing imported molasses. That brought forth the cry
that "taxation without representation is tyranny". Then
came the Stamp Act. When that was repealed, after the
merchants refused to import English goods and smug-
glers prospered, it was followed by import duties on

many articles, including tea. Again the colonies objected. Massachusetts called a Provincial Assembly; two regiments of British soldiers were stationed in Boston, and in 1770 came the "Boston Massacre" and a threat of a riot that forced the troops to move to barracks on islands in Boston harbor. The announcement that Massachusetts judges would henceforth be paid by the Crown brought about a Committee of Correspondence in Boston to inform all the other colonies of her troubles. Soon other colonies had their own Committees to exchange news and information.

Since the British East India Company was losing profits because it could not sell its tea in America, Parliament lowered the export duties so that tea could be sold cheaply, and a half-million pounds was sent to the four main ports in America. Two ports refused to allow the tea to be landed: at Charleston, customs men seized the tea ship because no one would pay the duty; at Boston, 15,000 pounds' worth was dumped in the harbor by a band of white men disguised as Indians. In the spring of 1774 the Boston Port Bill closed Boston to all commerce until the tea was paid for. Other acts practically annulled the colonial charter, abolished town meetings, and quartered soldiers in private houses. The Quebec Act extended Canada to the Ohio and wiped out the claims of several colonies to lands beyond the Alleghenies. In May, General Thomas Gage, now Governor of Massachusetts, came to Boston to enforce the acts. On June first, Boston, except for the narrow Boston Neck that connected the peninsula with the shore, was cut off from the world. Starvation threatened the people. Out of this threat and the need for common action grew the First Continental Congress that met in the fall in Philadelphia.

The colonies rallied to Boston's aid that summer. Charleston sent a shipload of rice that was unloaded at Marblehead and carried overland. Cattle were driven from all New England to the city. A thousand tons of wheat arrived from Quebec, and money came from Delaware. The village of Brooklyn in Connecticut gathered 120 sheep, and Israel Putnam volunteered to drive them to Boston. Announcing his arrival, the *Boston Gazette* called him "one of the greatest military characters of the age, a person whose bravery and character need no description, for he is so well known through North America that no words are necessary to inform the public any further concerning him than that his generosity led him to Boston to cherish the oppressed brethren and support them by every means in his power."

Wherever Putnam went, he found old friends and made new ones. On this trip he stayed for six weeks with young Dr. Joseph Warren. Blonde, blue-eyed, handsome, and dynamic, the young doctor had one of the best minds, and most effective pens, in Massachusetts. Each respected the other's abilities and they became devoted comrades.

There were many old friends in the British garrison in Boston, officers such as Lord Percy, Colonel John Small, and General Gage, who had marched and fought with Putnam and spent long evenings by Lake George, outside Havana, even around Detroit. In spite of the sheep for the colonists, the British were delighted to see him, and they entertained him at the taverns and on board ship. Inevitably, they swapped stories of the past and, tactfully, tried to look into the future.

During a convivial evening an officer asked him, "In case the dispute between the colonies and England should proceed to hostilities, what part, sir, would you take?"

"That of my country, sir, and whatever might happen I would be prepared to abide by the consequences."

In these talks, kept always cheerful and friendly by Putnam's good nature, the questions were sometimes more specific. On another occasion an officer asked, "Come now, sir, you have been a witness to the prowess and victories of the British fleets and armies. Do you not think them equal to the conquest of a country such as this, which does not own a single ship, regiment, or magazine of arms?"

"Well," replied Putnam with a wide smile, "I can only say that justice would be on our side, and, I should hope, Providence. But I have calculated that if it required six years for the combined forces of England and her colonies to conquer such a feeble country as Canada, it would, at least, take a very long time for England alone to overcome her own widely extended colonies, which are much stronger than Canada. Furthermore, sir, when men fight for everything that is dear to them, in what they believe to be the most sacred of all causes, and in their own native land, they would have great advantages over their enemies who are not in the same situation. Viewing all the circumstances, I, for my own part, fully believe that America would not be so easily conquered as you gentlemen seem to expect."

And once General Gage asked his old friend, "Do you not seriously believe, my friend, that a well-appointed British army of five thousand veterans could march through the whole continent of America?"

"No doubt, sir," Putnam agreed briskly, "if they behaved civilly, and paid well for everything they wanted." After a moment's pause he added, "But if they should attempt it in a hostile manner, and though the American men were out of the question, the women with their ladles and broomsticks would knock them all on the head before they got half way through."

This put an end to speculations that evening.

When he returned to Connecticut, Putnam urged the drilling of militia and the gathering of arms and ammunition. All over New England the village greens echoed with military commands, and powder, balls, and flints were stored in various secret places against the need that most men hoped would never arise. In the winter Putnam was made Lieutenant Colonel of the 11th Connecticut regiment.

One Thursday morning Putnam and his son Daniel, who was then fifteen, went to plow a field not far from the tavern. The date was April 20, 1775. At eight o'clock a messenger rode into the village with a copy of a letter from the Committee of Public Safety at Watertown in Massachusetts announcing the encounter between the British soldiers and the men of Lexington. Putnam dropped the plow, unhitched and mounted one of the horses of the team, and still in his work clothes rode to spread the news and consult with militia officers and with Governor Jonathan Trumbull at Lebanon. Trumbull ordered him to Boston to learn at first hand what had happened. When Putnam returned to Brooklyn two hours later another messenger had arrived with news of the fighting at Concord at the bridge and the harassing of the retreating British. Still in his checked farmer's smock, Putnam set out on a fresh horse for Cambridge. He rode a hundred miles in eighteen hours and arrived the next day.

All roads truly led to Boston in the days that followed, and all roads were filled with militia coming to fight the British. When they found there was no fighting at the moment, and because militia, who are civilians turning out in an emergency, never wish to be long from home, they melted away. The militia officers also departed, but many went to raise the 30,000 troops authorized by the Massachusetts Provincial Congress. They would return later with their own men.

The British, too, were reinforced, and by soldiers who stayed. Ships bringing 5,000 men arrived in Boston, along with a trio of Generals whose names would become well known on both sides of the Atlantic—Burgoyne, Clinton, and Howe, brother of the Lord Howe who had been killed at Ticonderoga and of Admiral Sir Richard Howe.

Samuel and John Adams and John Hancock, the most famous of the Massachusetts Whigs, were already in Philadelphia for the Second Continental Congress. Two days after Lexington, the Massachusetts Provincial Congress elected Dr. Joseph Warren its President. Warren, a friend of Paul Revere, had long been popular with the poor of Boston because he cared for them without pay, and with the middle-class and wealthy because of his intelligence and charm, his excellent family, and his delightful wife. But above all he had long been wholehearted in his devotion to the cause of freedom. He took over the chairmanship of the Committee of Correspondence and, what was vitally important, wrote the description of the events of the 18th of April. This went out to all the other colonies as the official version and so put the Massachusetts side of the fighting squarely on record for all to know.

A week later Putnam was called back to Connecticut to advise the General Assembly in special session at Hartford about the raising and provisioning of troops. The Assembly made him Brigadier General and his eldest son, Israel, a captain. Then Putnam was back in Cambridge where armies from the four New England colonies were settling down to watch the British in Boston. Artemus Ward, who had been on Abercrombie's disastrous expedition against Ticonderoga, was the general in command of the Massachusetts army, but no one knew whether he had any authority over the armies from the other colonies, and apparently he felt he did not. He asked Putnam to stay in Cambridge, although the rest of the Connecticut troops camped at Roxbury, so he might have him at hand for advice and support . . . and to share the responsibility. So Putnam, with his son Daniel and his aide, settled into the large square wooden house once owned by the Tory merchant John Borland, who had fled to Boston.

From the exceedingly narrow neck of land, the peninsula that held Boston extended in the shape of an irregular right-handed mitten face down in the harbor formed by the mouths of the Charles and Mystic rivers. On the landward end of the thin neck lay the village and low heights of Roxbury with the irregular peninsula of Dorchester, with its own heights, to the east and south of Boston and the harbor. To the west of Roxbury, beyond the village of Brookline and across the Charles, was the pleasant town of Cambridge two miles back from the shore. Directly opposite and north of the end of Boston, across a narrow strait, lay the pear-shaped peninsula of Charlestown, its broad base towards Boston. The village of Charlestown, where many of the wealthy families of Boston had sent their most valuable possessions for safe-keeping, was at the left-hand corner of the wide end of the peninsula. At the right-hand corner rose a low hill called Morton's. In the center of the peninsula amid stone-walled fields and orchards, rose a higher hill, Breed's, and behind that a slightly higher one called Bunker. A neck, so narrow it could carry only one road, led to the main shore, where stood three more hills between the Mystic to the north and the Charles to the south. The Provincial troops in the semicircle from the Mystic to Dorchester Heights effectively hemmed in the British.

Putnam persuaded General Ward that the heights of this semicircle should be fortified with entrenchments at once so that the militia could repel an attack at any spot and, he hoped, prevent the enemy's moving out into the country. The Massachusetts and Connecticut men were put to work throwing up breastworks and Putnam was constantly moving among them, on horseback or on foot. "His experience had taught him," wrote his son Dan later, "that raw and undisciplined troops must be employed in some way or other or they would soon become vicious and unmanageable. His maxim was 'it is better to dig a ditch every morning and fill it up at evening than to have the men idle.'" And along with Colonel William Prescott of Massachusetts, Putnam urged the fortifying of the heights on the Charlestown peninsula, but the Committee of Safety and the Provincial Congress felt this was too aggressive a move.

One day on a round of inspection Putnam came on some Massachusetts men sitting beside their pickaxes. "To what regiment do you belong?" he demanded.

"To Colonel Doolittle's," replied one of the men, not rising.

"Doolittle? Do nothing at all!" exclaimed the General angrily, and he galloped away.

But not all his time was devoted to overseeing the entrenchments. Dr. Warren spent as much time as he could at the Borland house discussing military strategy and tactics with the veteran and listening to his wartime experiences. Warren was particularly concerned about the quality of the Provincial troops in comparison with that of the British regulars. Putnam always maintained that when the Provincial regiments were well officered they were not inferior. "Our men," he said, "would always follow wherever their officers led. I know this to have been the case with mine, and I have seen it in other instances."

"But if ten thousand British troops should march out of Boston what number do you believe, General, would be competent to meet them?"

"Let me pick my officers and I would not fear to meet them with half that number. Not in a pitched battle, mind you, to stop them at once. No troops are better than the British. But I would fight on the retreat from behind every stone wall we passed. Our men are lighter of foot, they know our grounds and how to take advantage of them. Besides, we should only fall back on our reserves while every step they advanced the country would close on their flanks and rear."

"And," he would repeat in defense of the ditches that

were being dug on the hills around Cambridge, "Americans are not afraid of their heads. They are very much afraid of their legs. Cover their legs and they will fight until doomsday."

But he also knew that digging ditches alone would not sustain the morale of the troops. On May 13 he marched all except those on guard from Cambridge to the Charlestown peninsula, over Bunker Hill, down the ridge to the lower but steeper Breed's Hill, through the village and back along the road by the water. The British ships sat in a row and watched them, waiting for the shot that never came.

It came some two weeks later in the form of a confused skirmish. The islands of Boston harbor had long fed the city with the cattle and wheat grown on them. The British began to move cattle from the islands into the city, for they were short of fresh meat. The Provincials decided to stop them, and waded at low tide to Hog Island and began to drive off the livestock. The British navy had hidden stores on nearby Noodle Island, so Admiral Graves sent the schooner *Diana* to guard them. When the marines landed, the Americans volleyed and then drove the sheep, cows, and horses toward the shore. Gage sent more marines to help the *Diana,* but by now the *Diana,* unable to move against wind and tide, was drifting toward the American shore.

Next the British sent a sloop and barges to pull her off. The Americans had sent for help. In an hour General Putnam, Dr. Warren, and a thousand men arrived. Though the *Diana* continued to drift she refused to surrender. The British and Americans fired at each other, but at too great range to do much damage. At one point

78

Putnam led his men waist-deep into the water and mud so their shots would take more effect. At dusk the *Diana* grounded and was abandoned by her crew. At dawn the Americans removed everything that could be pried loose and set her afire for all Boston to see. When the armed sloop came back for another fight, she was so riddled with shot she had to be towed away. Not an American was killed. This engagement sent the army's spirits up like a rocket, and the news was carried far and wide and even to Philadelphia. Putnam became more famous than ever, because he had led the fight and the Americans had come out of it victorious.

In spite of the bullets, many of the British officers were still friends. An exchange of prisoners was finally arranged in early June, and Putnam and Warren escorted them, with a troop from Connecticut, to the ferry at Charlestown. The British exchange party was under Major Small and Major Moncrieff. When they disbarked from the schooner *Lively* and Moncrieff and Putnam saw each other, they ran into each other's arms and kissed on both cheeks, to the great diversion and astonishment of the American soldiers. After the wounded were put on board the schooner, the four officers moved to the house of a Doctor Foster for luncheon and so enjoyed themselves that the British stayed two hours longer than was expected. A few days later, hearing that Mrs. Gage and her family were short of meat, Putnam sent her a fine quarter of veal under a flag of truce.

Putnam pointed out to young Dan that Gage's exchange of prisoners carried real meaning. "He may call us Rebels now, if he will, but why then don't he hang his prisoners instead of exchanging them? By this act he has virtually placed us on an equality and acknowledged our right of resistance." Gage made another gesture of meaning also. Somehow he got word to Putnam that if he would abandon the rebels' party he would be made a Major General in the British army with a more than generous compensation for his military services to the Crown. Putnam ignored the offer and kept it a secret for many years.

On June 10th Putnam took his men on another march to Charlestown and back, and Dan proudly marched with them. The next evening Putnam had a long talk with Colonel Prescott. He was a taciturn farmer from Pepperell (a village on the coast beyond New Hampshire), who had distinguished himself in the campaign of 1759 against Louisbourg and then returned to farming, reading military histories, and drilling the militia. Both men preferred action to debate. Afterwards, Dan reported, his father fell into an old habit of talking to himself when he was thinking deeply. Several times he heard the General muttering such things as "we must go there" . . . "they will come out" . . . . "we must go in the night" . . . . "have a trench before morning" . . . . "I know them, they fire without aim" . . . Dan could only listen and wonder.

There was debate at a Council of War at the headquarters of General Ward three nights later. Trustworthy information had been brought from Boston that Gage was planning within a few days to seize both Dorchester Heights to the southeast and the peninsula of Charlestown to the northwest to break the siege of the city and make sure the rebels had no near ground from which to attack. What, if anything, should the Americans do?

"We must draw the enemy from Boston to where we can meet them on equal terms," Putnam maintained. "Charlestown and Dorchester are the only places this could be done. We must fortify Bunker Hill and the mainland behind it."

"We have no powder to spare and no cannon," Ward pointed out.

"The army needs to be employed," said Putnam, "and the country is dissatisfied with its inactivity. We must do something."

"But it might bring on a general action," someone protested.

"We could cripple their army," Putnam told the council forcefully. "Two thousand men of ours are all we should risk. We would defend ourselves as long as we can and then give ground. But we must fight behind cover on ground in our favor."

"But if the retreat is intercepted?"

"We can run when we can contend no more. We can out-run them and turn and halt them."

"But suppose we are hemmed in and there is no retreat?"

"We know what we are fighting for. We will set our country an example of which it shall not be ashamed and show those who seek to oppress us what men can do who are determined to live free or not at all." He spoke with passionate conviction.

Dr. Warren's blue eyes glowed. As head of the Committee of Safety and President of the Provincial Congress he had the greatest authority at the council, and the greatest responsibility. His assent would be necessary for any action.

Though fired, he spoke slowly. "Almost you persuade me, General Putnam. I still think the project rash. Nevertheless, if it should be adopted and the strife becomes hard you must not be surprised to find me in the midst of it."

"I hope not," Putnam answered earnestly, and perhaps he remembered young Lord Howe below Ticonderoga. "You are a young man and our country has much to hope from you, both in council and in war. Let some of us who are older and can well enough be spared begin the fight."

On June 15th the Committee of Safety resolved that possession should be taken of the hill called Bunker on Charlestown peninsula, to be held and defended, and also some hill or hills on Dorchester Heights. The Council of War immediately approved. But General Thomas, in command at Roxbury, when told of the plan by Putnam, called his own council of war of his own troops. That council refused to occupy Dorchester Heights or take any part in the joint operation. So the opportunity of action on both flanks to confuse the British was lost. But the fortifying of Bunker Hill was urged again by Putnam and by Prescott. This was at last approved, and Prescott was directed to fortify Bunker Hill by a strong redoubt with cannon planted to annoy the enemy if they should come out of Charlestown village or go up the Mystic to Medford.

"Putnam's regiment was under arms," wrote Daniel, "and I was informed by the Adjutant that a detachment had been made from it for secret service. But what at the time impressed my mind most strongly was the preparations my father himself was making. With his own hands he prepared cartridges for his pistols, took out the old flints, and put in the new. While he was doing this Colonel Prescott came in and observing what he was about, said in a low tone, "I see, General, you are making preparation and we shall be ready at the time."

"A little after sunset my father called me aside and said, "You will go to Mrs. Inman's (the farm that was the headquarters for the Connecticut officers) as usual tonight, and it is time you were gone. You need not return here in the morning, but stay there tomorrow; the family may want you. And if they find it necessary to leave the house you must go with them where they go; and try now, my son, to be as serviceable to them as you can.'

"This order left me no doubt in my mind that some military movement was going forward in which my father was to participate. With earnest endeavor I asked leave to accompany him. 'You, dear father,' I said, 'may need my assistance much more than Mrs Inman; pray let me go where you are going.'

" 'No, no, Daniel, do as I have bid you,' was the answer which he affected to give sternly, while his voice trembled and his eyes filled. He added 'You can do little, my son, where I am going, and besides, there will be enough to take care of me.' "

Daniel obeyed. (The next afternoon he went into the fields when he heard the sound of distant shooting, and says he thought of disobeying his father. But Mrs Inman begged him to stay and protect her and her daughters in case the British came, so he stayed, through the long day.)

For the fortifying of Bunker Hill, Prescott's own regiment was chosen and also two other Massachusetts regiments and 200 from Putnam's Connecticut regiment under his favorite captain, Thomas Knowlton . . . about 1200 men in all. Captain Samuel Gridley's Massachusetts Artillery Company, men of no experience, were to go along with two field pieces. The troops paraded at six in the evening on the night of June 16th on Cambridge common. President Samuel Langdon of Harvard College offered a prayer. All the entrenching tools in camp were gathered and provisions for 24 hours. None of the soldiers knew where they were going.

Chapter Seven

"Don't Fire Until You See
the Whites of Their Eyes"

IN THE DUSK the soldiers marched from Cambridge Common to Charlestown Neck following the tall figure of Colonel Prescott wearing a light blue coat and black tricorn hat. The wagon with the entrenching tools followed the men. At the narrow road on the neck, between the Mystic and a millpond, which joined the apex of the triangular peninsula to the shore, Putnam was waiting on his white horse. The troops were halted and ordered to load their muskets with two balls while the officers explained to the men what they were about to do and why. One company was sent to guard Charlestown. The rest followed Putnam up and over Bunker Hill, a round hill 110 feet high that rose half a mile from the neck, and on to a ridge that connected that hill with the lower but steeper Breed's Hill. Here the men halted again.

Followed by the officers, behind two men with dark lanterns, Putnam and Prescott climbed Breed's Hill.

With them was Colonel Richard Gridley, the most famous of the New England engineers, whose skill had enabled Wolfe's men to drag two cannon up straight cliffs to the Plains of Abraham and capture Quebec. The Committee and General Ward had said to occupy and fortify Bunker Hill. Someone pointed out that Breed's was sometimes called Bunker's. Another insisted that it was more important. Putnam maintained that Bunker was too far from the harbor for any cannon to reach the British ships, and that with its steep slope to the south and east Breed's could be better defended. They moved along the crest still arguing until Colonel Gridley pointed out that it was midnight, with only four hours remaining to dawn. From the engineering point of view, he agreed, Breed's was the more satisfactory to fortify. Prescott still hesitated. Putnam had no authority over Massachusetts men, for his rank of Brigadier was in the Connecticut militia, but he had long experience and prestige, and Gridley was renowned. Putnam pointed out also that Bunker Hill should be fortified in case Breed's had to be evacuated. At last Prescott agreed that they would begin with Breed's Hill.

With a pickax Gridley began to draw lines in the dirt where the redoubt was to be made. It was to be oblong, 160 feet long and half as wide, with walls (six feet high and a foot and a half thick) and a firing platform for the soldiers to stand on inside. Already men were lugging up bundles of fascines and empty hogsheads to be filled with dirt and packed into the earthworks. Muskets were stacked and the men began to dig, half an hour on and half an hour off. For the most part they were farmers in long, loose home-dyed coats, leather trousers that fastened below the knee, woolen stockings, and cowhide shoes. They were used to digging, but it was exhausting work. Prescott threw off his coat and hat and led the officers in digging beside the men. In the starshine across the flickering water lay the black humpy mass that was Boston, and between swung three blots that were British ships. Putnam, on his horse, his sword at his belt, set off for Cambridge to ask General Ward to send food and water for the men and reinforcements to relieve them at digging.

At dawn several things happened. Prescott realized that his left flank was unprotected and started the men digging a breastwork north from the redoubt toward the swamp by the Mystic. He sent another regiment to deserted Charlestown village. One man on the British sloop *Lively,* anchored opposite Breed's Hill in the river, noticed the brown splash of dirt against the green of the hillside. The Captain of the *Lively* opened fire. Boston town awoke. The soldiers digging behind the earthen wall dropped shovels and ran to watch the cannonballs fall short at the bottom of the hill. It was the first cannon many of them had ever heard. They became uneasy and Prescott, talking calmly, walked among them as they worked. Gridley urged more work on the breastwork on the left flank. In Cambridge Putnam went to remind General Ward again that refreshments and men must be sent to Charlestown Heights as planned or the whole expedition would fail; then on a fresh horse he galloped to join the men on the hill.

The sun rose red beyond the blue water of the harbor. It would be a hot, oppressive day. The second round of shot from the *Lively* went over the redoubt, the third crashed into the sides of the parapet and bounced off downhill. Without thought, the men dropped their picks and crouched. "Keep digging!" shouted Prescott and seized a shovel. "Keep digging. They can't hurt us here."

The other two ships, the *Somerset* and the *Falcon,* opened, followed by the battery on Copp's Hill at the tip of Boston peninsula. One cannonball took off a man's head. Prescott ordered him buried without prayers. There might have been panic then, but Prescott, now in a long brown coat, climbed to the top of the parapet and strolled along, talking to the captain who followed him. Putnam found the weary men, seven free Negroes among them, already suffering from the heat and exertion. There was no water and little ammunition, and they had been digging for six hours. In his shirt sleeves now, with an old white felt hat on his curly gray hair, he mounted his horse and set out again for Cambridge and General Ward. Prescott ordered the regiment to come back from Charlestown.

In Province House in Boston the British generals were holding a Council of War. Governor Gage, who had spent eighteen years in the colonies and married a handsome American wife, sat at the head of the table, with Lord Howe, General John Burgoyne, who had refused to believe 10,000 peasants could hold 5,000 of His Majesty's troops immobile, General Sir Henry Clinton, and Brigadier General Earl Percy, who had commanded the retreat from Lexington and had already altered his opinions about the fighting abilities of those same peasants. Clinton maintained that a force of troops could be rowed to Charlestown Neck, land, and take the Provincials in the rear. Burgoyne and Percy agreed, but Gage held it too hazardous a maneuver, for then the British would be between two armies. With Howe, he felt a frontal attack was the only possible one, for the farmers on the hill would never stand against the regulars. A show of force would be all that was needed. The Tory General Ruggles warned them the British would be slaughtered and, when ignored, stalked out to join the crowds on the tops of the houses. Because of the tide, the troops could not embark until noon.

In Cambridge Putnam was finding General Ward still reluctant to commit more troops to the fight, for he was afraid the British would land to create a diversion and attack Cambridge. Finally he agreed to order half of General John Stark's New Hampshire regiment to join Prescott's men. But the available bullets would not fit the muskets, and Stark's men spent two hours pounding lead balls by hand to make them the right size. They had 15 rounds to a man. It took so long to persuade the Committee and Ward and Warren that it was 10 o'clock before Putnam started back to Breed's Hill. On the way he passed Major Brook, on foot because there were no horses, bringing another request from Prescott for water, ammunition, and men.

At the redoubt the men cheered Putnam, and he shouted praise for all they had accomplished. For two months he had done his best by hard work and force of example and without much help to turn raw militia into an army with some pride and courage. Soon it would be evident whether he had had any success at all. He told the perspiring, dusty, tired men that Ward had promised both reinforcements and refreshments. The extension of the breastworks to the left had been finished. When Putnam saw the entrenching tools stacked back of the redoubt, he told Prescott they should be carried to Bunker Hill and the digging should be begun there for the second line of defense, as agreed, in case the redoubt had to be abandoned.

"If the men take the tools to the other hill, not one will have the courage to return," said Prescott.

"They shall every man return," Putnam told him stoutly. He spoke to some of his own Connecticut men nearby. "My lads, these tools must be carried back." His voice reached other troops who jumped to seize the tools and race down the slope.

For once Putnam was largely wrong, for many of the men never did return to the redoubt. But, following to Bunker Hill, he got the men there to start throwing up a breastwork. Some of the tools, however, were carried as far as Cambridge. By now the British ships were firing not only on the redoubt, but also with flaming fire balls and had set fire to the houses of Charlestown. The two gunboats and the *Glasgow* had moved toward the Charles and were enfilading Charlestown Neck. Again Putnam rode to Cambridge to see where the ammunition, men, and "refreshments" were. At Boston the British regiments were beginning to embark.

General Ward had been persuaded to let all the New Hampshire men and some from Massachusetts go to the peninsula. Putnam sent for his own Connecticut troops. The first British scows came to shore on Morton's Point. Prescott, sure they would attack on his left flank, sent Captain Thomas Knowlton and the Connecticut men who had come with him originally toward the shore with two small cannon. Putnam rode up to them and led them to a fence of rails set in front of a low stone wall that was parallel to and slightly to the rear of the redoubt on Breed's Hill and ran almost from that hill to the Mystic. There was an apple orchard in front, and in a nearby field the hay had just been mowed. The men stacked their arms and went to work gathering hay, bushes, clumps of earth, and rails from another fence to put between fence and wall, thus giving an air of solidity to the fence. The guns were set at the right end next to the base of the hill.

Colonel Stark, an old comrade of Putnam's who had been a captain with Rogers' Rangers, and Colonel Reed were leading the New Hampshire men to Bunker Hill when Putnam galloped to him.

"Push on, Colonel Stark. The enemy have landed and formed," cried Putnam, and he waved toward the fence. Its importance was obvious. Stark turned the men there and set some to building a stone wall on the beach, from the bank to the water, to forestall flanking. Captain Callender and his artillery were sent to the space between fence and hill. Colonel Gridley took some men and began to dig small "fleches," V-shaped little forts of rails and dirt, on the side of the hill so an attack on the rail fence could be enfiladed. The sun was hotter than ever. The guns of the ships boomed steadily. On the far shore, soldiers in red coats and white trousers were opening knapsacks for lunch.

About to start for Cambridge once more, Putnam met Dr. Joseph Warren coming down the slope of Bunker Hill. Warren was dressed in his best: black suit, pale-blue waistcoat laced with silver, white ruffled shirt, white satin knee breeches, a sword at his side and a musket on his shoulder. Three days before, he had been appointed a major general in the Massachusetts army, but his commission had not come through.

Putnam dismounted. "I am sorry to see you here, General Warren," he said. "I wish you had taken my advice and left this day to us, for we shall have a sharp time of it. Since you are here, I am ready to submit to your orders."

"No, no," Warren protested. "I came only as a volunteer. I know nothing of your dispositions, nor will I interfere with them. Tell me where I can be most useful."

Pointing to the redoubt, Putnam told him, "You will be covered there."

"Do not think I came to seek a place of safety," Warren said. "Tell me where the onset will be most furious."

Again Putnam pointed to the redoubt. "That is the enemy's object. Prescott is there and will do his duty. If it can be defended the day is ours."

Warren nodded and walked toward the redoubt. Cheers burst from all the men behind the earthen wall as, calm and smiling, he joined them. They felt that if the President of the Provincial Congress had come to join the fight it was an important one, and in spite of fatigue more than one back straightened, and thirst and heat and apprehension were briefly forgotten. Prescott stepped down from the firing platform and offered him the command. Warren shook his head. "I came as a volunteer to serve under you. I shall be happy to learn from a soldier of your experience."

There was another volunteer cheered by the men. Seth Pomeroy of Northampton, sixty-eight years old, who had said in 1755 that the British retreat before the French at Lake George was a handsome one, had ridden from home to Cambridge without pausing and onto Charlestown Neck. Seeing the shots sweeping over that narrow strip, he had dismounted and asked a man to lead the horse to safety, since it was borrowed, and then, shouldering the prized musket he had carried 30 years before at the siege of Louisbourg, strode through the shot to the redoubt.

"By God," Putnam shouted when he saw his old friend. "Pomeroy! You here! A cannon shot would waken you out of your grave."

It was three in the afternoon; 3,000 British troops had landed on the peninsula, had beef, biscuits, and rum, and rested. Now half a mile away, they were forming to advance. Howe was trusting the Americans would be terrified at the solid advancing lines beneath the glittering bayonets, would fire a few shots, and run. His tactics were practical and simple. The marines under Pitcairn would move through burning Charlestown and attack the redoubt from the south; the regulars would make a frontal attack on the redoubt. The grenadiers, the tallest men in the army, made a foot higher by their bearskin hats, would advance on the rail fence while the light infantry, moving quickly down the beach, with bayonets would scatter the men at the stone wall and come on the Americans from the rear. All the British soldiers carried knapsacks with food for three days, blanket rolls, muskets, powder and balls, extra clothing and canteen, to a weight of a hundred pounds.

The red-and-white lines started forward, but the green land before them was deep in grass, criss-crossed with stone and rail fences, which disrupted the orderly march; in part it was so swampy the artillery bogged down. Two small ponds broke the advance for several minutes. The sea wind was beginning to blow away the black smoke from the burning houses of Charlestown where the marines were already having trouble with snipers. General Pigot led the attack up the hill. Howe was leading the grenadiers against the rail fence. "I shall not desire any of you to advance a single step beyond where I am at the head of the line," he had told the troops.

Half a mile away all Boston was watching.

At the rail fence the soldiers rested their guns on the top rail. Putnam rode up and down behind them, pausing once to beat a man back into position with the flat of his sword. "Men," he told them conversationally, "you are all marksmen. Don't fire until you see the whites of their eyes. Powder is low. Don't waste it."

"Fire low," said Stark and Knowlton and Reed. "Aim at the waistbands. Aim at their gaiters. Any one of you could kill a squirrel at a hundred yards."

Up on the redoubt, Prescott walked along the parapet. "Don't fire until I tell you," he told the men behind the dirt wall. "Aim at the handsomest coats. Powder is scarce. Keep your heads." With his sword he pushed up a musket. "Wait."

The first attack was along the beach against the stone wall where Stark and the New Hampshire men waited. The light infantry (Howe had led them in the climb up the cliffs beside the St. Lawrence at Quebec) came quickly and confidently. At 15 paces the stone wall burst into a sheet of red flame that dropped all but a handful. The second regiment, plowing over the dead and wounded, met with another annihilating blast. The third advanced and was mowed down, and the survivors fled.

A little later than planned, Howe and the grenadiers

advanced toward the rail fence: grenadiers and regulars under General Pigot moved on the redoubt. It was very hot and the sun was bright on the red coats; it glinted on brass buckles, whitened the white breeches, and shone on the gold gorgets at the officers' throats. Drums and fifes beat and shrilled on the flanks. The laden soldiers, already weary from climbing fences, were sweating. But they came on, and the Americans waited in silence.

In one movement the bayonets were lowered for the charge, 30 yards away. "Fire!" thundered Putnam behind the rail fence. "Fire!" shouted Prescott behind the parapet. A solid line of red flame sent the British troops down in windrows, crumbling, staggering, falling. The second line fell, and the third. For a moment Howe stood alone in front of the fence, his officers and men fallen around him. "A moment I never felt before," he said later. Not a man fired at him. He and the few survivors retreated. As his third wave fell, Pigot gave the same order.

Putnam was having his own troubles with the field pieces standing in the gap between the hill and the fence. "General Putnam came to one of the pieces near which I stood," said one soldier, "and furiously enquired where our officers were. (They and most of the men had left the post.) On being told our cartridges were too big and the pieces could not be loaded he swore and said they could be. Taking a cartridge he broke it open and loaded the pieces with a ladle . . ." and sprinkled powder at the touchhole and put a match to it. If the powder had flared back, he could have lost an arm. His first ball went high; the barrel of one cannon burst; a double handful of musket balls from the other tore a gap in the ranks of the advancing grenadiers, but the ranks filled. There was more for him to do than help in the firing of the cannon. Three men at the rail fence fired without orders. Putnam hurried there. "General Putnam appeared to be very angry," wrote a soldier, "and passed along the lines quickly with his sword drawn and threatened to stab any man that fired without orders. The enemy kept firing as they advanced, and when they got pretty near the works we were all ordered to take good aim and fire. All this time General Putnam was constantly passing backwards and forwards from right to left telling us the day was ours if we would only stick to it."

In the pause after the retreat Putnam rode to Bunker Hill. On the way he encountered Captain Callender of the artillery and some of his men. "He ordered the officer to go back. He replied he had no cartridges. The General dismounted and examined his boxes and found a considerable number of cartridges, upon which he ordered him back. He refused until the General threatened him with immediate death, upon which he returned." But he and his men did not stay long. Putnam found the field pieces at the foot of the hill and asked a Massachusetts company to draw them to the front. They refused at first, but when their own captain made an impassioned speech they seized the draw-ropes and drew the guns to the rail fence, and at last some volunteers took over.

General Clinton and General Burgoyne were watching through their spyglasses from the top of Copp's Hill. Every roof and window and tree in Boston was black with people watching aghast. Charlestown was burning furiously; the men-of-war and the floating batteries were sending shots steadily toward the center hill and across

Charlestown Neck. On the slope of the hill, now brown from the dirt flung up by cannonballs, on the beach and the fields lay a heavy carpet of red-and-white. From that carpet the regulars were running back to their barges.

General Burgoyne described what he saw in a letter to a friend in England a few days later.

"And now ensued one of the greatest scenes of war that can be conceived . . . Straight before us a large and noble town in one great blaze. The church steeples being of timber were great pyramids of fire above the rest . . . the roar of cannon, mortars and musketry, the crash of churches, ships upon the stocks, and whole streets falling together in ruins fill the air; the storm of the redoubt . . . made the whole a picture and a complication of horror and importance beyond anything that ever came to my lot to be a witness."

Clinton left the hill and raced for a boat and joined Howe and Pigot as they were re-forming their lines. Howe was limping from a wound in his foot. Some of the remaining officers were in favor of Clinton's plan to bring ships and men to take the Neck. Howe said no. The honor of the British army was at stake. It was inconceivable they would not ultimately carry the day.

Putnam rode to Bunker Hill, where he knew breast-works would be needed if Breed's was lost, and found the work slow. The men trickling across Charlestown Neck were chiefly officers who were simply leaving behind the men who refused to cross amid the cannonballs and chain shot. Putnam raced to the chaos on the shore. He entreated the men to follow him; he threatened to shoot those who did not, and finally, to show there was no danger from the firing from the ships, he rode his horse back and forth across the Neck through the hottest fire. The balls threw up dirt around him, but not one hit him or his horse. This merely convinced the soldiers he was invulnerable—but not that they were. At last a few troops followed him across. At Bunker Hill he tried to rally the men who had already reached the west side, where they were protected, ordering and entreating them forward into the lines of the fences and the redoubt. But they said they had no officers, and anyway he was not one of theirs, they were Massachusetts men.

Putnam gave up and hurried to the rail fence. The British were advancing, over the fields and the fences and across their own dead and wounded, firing as they marched. The Americans waited until the blue facing on the red coats of the grenadiers was clear and the distance twenty yards.

"I saw General Putnam," said a Connecticut private who was at the breastwork of green grass, "riding along the whole line and shouting, 'Stick to your posts, men. Do your duty'. He was greatly exposed."

Whole platoons went down when the Americans fired. "General Putnam encouraged us very much," said another soldier. "He rode up and down behind us, his horse all of a lather. The battle was going very hotly. One of the regiment got down behind a haycock. General Putnam rode up and cried 'God's curse on him. Run him through if he won't fight.' He gave the man one or two whacks with his sword and drove him to the ranks. He did much to keep us steady."

Three times the British came on, fell and withdrew, and at last retreated. "By God," Putnam cried as he saw them go down, "I never saw such a carnage of the human race."

Major John Small of the 47th regiment had his own escape from death. "I, with the other officers, was in the front of the line to encourage the men; we had advanced very near the works, undisturbed, when an irregular fire was poured upon us; it was cruelly fatal. The troops fell back, and when I looked to the right and left I saw not one officer standing. I glanced my eye to the enemy and saw several young men levelling their pieces at me; I knew their excellence as marksmen and I considered myself gone. At that moment my old friend Putnam rushed forward and striking up the muzzles of their pieces with his sword cried out, 'For God's sake, my lads, don't fire at that man. I love him as I do my brother.' We were so near to each other that I heard his words distinctly. He was obeyed. I bowed and thanked him and walked away unmolested."

Among the British carried from the field was Lieutenant General Abercrombie, who fell mortally wounded at the head of his grenadiers. As he passed a fellow officer he called out, "If you take General Putnam alive, don't hang him. He's a brave man."

In the pause of the second retreat, Putnam again on his weary white horse galloped back toward the Neck. Some troops were beginning to cross at last and Putnam urged —commanded—them to go to the heights of Bunker Hill to entrench, to prepare for the enemy. "Press on. Press on. Our brethren are suffering and will be cut off," he shouted. "The musket balls flew very thick where Putnam was," reported a soldier, "nearly on or quite on top of Bunker Hill. He did not seem to mind it. He had a sword in his hand and hallooed to us to drive us up." Gardner's Massachusetts men climbed the hill.

The attack on the redoubt had been delayed and harassed by the men who had been in Charlestown and were now retreating. Some of them joined the handful at a small stone fence and forced Pigot to send his marines against them, deflecting a battalion from the hill itself. But the red ranks advanced. On this side they suffered fewer casualties than Howe's troops because the Americans were firing downhill and aim is more difficult. In the third British attack the first volley again halted the advancing troops. Again Prescott and Warren had held the men from firing and the men had obeyed willingly. The supply of balls was low in every pouch, perhaps three to a man. Some gathered up nails and pebbles for the muskets. Others had stacked stones at hand. Walking among the men, Warren and Prescott had assured them that if they could send the British back one more time the day was theirs.

The firing at the second line was thin. Confidence surged back into the redcoats. They began to climb the parapet on three sides, bayonets leveled. Some sergeants were shouting, "Conquer or die."

"Twitch their guns," roared Prescott. "Use your muskets as clubs."

The marines came over the west parapet unhindered. Prescott had sworn he would never be taken alive, and he parried bayonets with his sword until he saw the fight was lost. "Give way, men," he shouted. "Save yourselves." Still parrying, the press of the retiring men carried him out of the back of the redoubt. Warren gathered a group at the exit and held back the British with clubs and muskets until most of the Americans had escaped. Then the group began to back slowly through the gap and down the hill.

Desperately Warren called to them to make a stand. The British formed and volleyed, and Warren fell, shot through the head.

From Bunker Hill Putnam saw the Americans retreating. Waving Gardner's men forward he galloped down the hill and back and forth among the retreating men. "Make a stand here!" he shouted, swinging his sword, his face red with rage. "We can stop them yet! One more shot!" But the men kept on retreating. Seth Pomeroy waved his smashed musket over his head, begged the men to halt. But there were no more bullets. Gardner's men spread out and from behind what walls and bushes were available kept up a steady fire and held back the British. This enabled many of the retreating men to escape. Gardner himself had fallen. When his son begged permission to carry him to the rear, Gardner ordered him to return to the fight. Stark and Knowlton were bringing their men back in orderly retreat, with the British held back by some fresh troops, when the enemy cannon opened on them, causing many casualties.

By the unfinished trenches on the top of Bunker Hill Putnam on his horse still pleaded with the flying men to stand. It was as if they did not hear him. He rode down to an abandoned field piece and dismounted to fight alone. One Connecticut sergeant stayed with him to protect him. Putnam had loaded, the British were ten paces away, the sergeant fell dead. At last Putnam mounted and turned to Charlestown Neck. Here fresh troops and exhausted veterans were hopelessly mingled, but he found half his own regiment. He would lead them, and some others, for a counterattack. But a British gun commenced firing from Bunker Hill. Putnam rode across the Neck once more and calmly examined the cannon and their position. If more were brought, they could annihilate the retreating Americans. So, instead, he returned and led the men who would follow to Prospect Hill on the Cambridge road and ordered them to continue to fortify it, in case the British should follow to the mainland.

Then he rode to headquarters to join Prescott in demanding fresh troops for a counterattack against the weary British. Ward felt it unwise and refused. The British might still attack Cambridge, even though they were too weary to follow the men across the Neck. He still held 7,000 fresh men at Roxbury because Lord Percy was bombarding, as he had all afternoon, from Boston Neck, and Ward feared an attack there.

So, instead of leading a counterattack, Putnam returned to his men. They dug all night until dawn, when Ward sent a thousand reinforcements, and on into the day. Daniel Putnam went to see his father early Sunday morning. "I found him on the morning of the 18th of June about ten o'clock on Prospect Hill, dashing about among the workmen, throwing up entrenchments and often seizing a shovel or placing a sod with his own hands. He wore the same clothes he had on when I left him on the 16th."

At three o'clock that afternoon a thunderstorm silenced the cannon on both sides.

The British in the fight on the Charlestown peninsula had lost over 1,100 men, nearly half the attacking force, and nearly half their officers were killed or wounded. The Americans lost about 400. Their greatest loss was the intelligence, the courage, the inspiration, of Dr. Joseph Warren. But their greatest gain was in the shock to the

British army and to the people and government in England, and in the tremendous lift to the morale of the colonies. Untrained civilians had stood and thrown back the best of England's soldiers twice, and in the end had been defeated only because of lack of powder and shot. It was incredible. But since it had been accomplished once, it could be done again.

For a while, in later years, it became fashionable to decry Israel Putnam and the part he played on June 17th. But Washington Irving, in his *Life of Washington,* sums up the general and the enduring feeling.

"Putnam also was a leading spirit throughout the affair; one of the first to prompt and one of the last to maintain it. He appears to have been active and efficient at every point; sometimes fortifying; sometimes hurrying up reinforcements; inspiriting the men by his presence while they were able to maintain their ground, and fighting gallantly at the outpost to cover their retreat. The brave old man, riding about in the heat of the action, on this sultry day, 'with a hanger belted across his brawny shoulders, over a waistcoat without sleeves,' has been sneered at by a contemporary as much fitter to head a band of sickle men or ditchers than musketeers.' But this very description illustrates his character and identifies him with the times and the service. A yeoman fresh from the plough, in the garb of rural labour; a patriot brave and generous, but rough and ready, who thought not of himself in time of danger but was ready to serve in any way, and to sacrifice official rank and self-glorification to the good of the cause. He was eminently a soldier for the occasion. His name has long been a favorite one with young and old; one of the talismanic names of the Revolution, the very mention of which is like the sound of a trumpet. Such names are the precious jewels of our history, to be garnered up among the treasures of the nation, and kept immaculate from the tarnishing breath of the cynic and the doubter."

Chapter Eight

The Unanimous Choice of Congress

THE BRITISH THREW UP their own entrenchments on Bunker Hill and stayed there. The Americans went on fortifying their hills around Cambridge, Roxbury, and Dorchester, for General Ward still believed there might be an attack at any moment, and he released more troops to build forts and breastworks under Putnam's direction. Once more the General was back on his white horse, appearing to judge the work when least expected.

A soldier named Harvey said, "On one occasion General Putnam came along near where I was at work and seeing a quantity of sods which had just been brought up he addressed himself to one of the men, directing him to place them on the wall, remarking at the same time, 'You are a soldier, I suppose?' The order not being executed on the instant the General added, 'Oh, I see you are an officer!' and immediately took hold and placed the sods himself. Meanwhile the balls were continually pouring in from the British forts, sometimes killing our men and sometimes tearing our works, but they went forward nevertheless, and soon were in a condition to return the compliment."

Soon these fortifications were to be inspected by the new Commander-in-Chief, for on June 14th, at the wise urging of John Adams, a Virginia militia colonel named George Washington had been appointed to that rank by the Continental Congress. When, five days later, word of the engagement reached Philadelphia, Washington and his staff set out for Boston. In spite of his desire to hurry, he was greeted with speeches and banquets at practically every town through which he passed. On Sunday, July 2nd, in the early afternoon, after a trip of ten days, he arrived in Cambridge and was escorted to the house of the President of Harvard, who was left with one room for his family of seven. The officers who greeted him there saw a tall, handsome, reddish-haired, blue-eyed man, meticulously uniformed, who looked the part of the commander of an army more than that of the pleasant Virginia squire. Ponderous and cool to this stranger, General Ward made the introductions. Israel Putnam had been the only one of the four major generals named to the Continental army by Congress who received an unanimous vote, and Washington handed him then the paper that gave him that rank. Putnam was openly pleased and accepted it with obvious pleasure.

The three other major generals were Charles Lee, who had accompanied Washington, Artemus Ward, and Philip Schuyler of New York. Horatio Gates was Adjutant. Nine brigadier generals had also been chosen. The next morning Washington, surrounded by his officers, rode to Cambridge Common where the troops were drawn up; there he formally assumed command of the Continental army and went immediately to inspect the posts and entrenchments on the nearby hills.

Prospect Hill was the highest, and from there he could see the whole of Boston Bay, its peninsulas and islands and marshes, the blue waters crowded with ships, the town and its church steeples bright in the afternoon sun. If the British attacked, or were to be attacked, it would have to be from the peninsulas of Charlestown, which they held, or Dorchester or Roxbury where there were American posts. The extremely narrow neck that led to Boston itself was fortified and held by the enemy, but with the Americans rimming the harbor, they were held immobile. After learning the state of the army, the lack of clothes, shoes, guns, ammunition, cannon and shelter, it became evident that Washington's task would be to hold the British in place while he tried to build an army. That army continued to melt away as the Minutemen returned home and militia went back to their fields.

When the brigadier generals were announced Seth Pomeroy, disappointed and angry at holding a lesser rank than Putnam, went home to Northampton. Some others also left camp, though some returned. As one officer wrote, "Better for us to lose four Spencers than half a Putnam. Generals Washington and Lee are vastly fonder and think higher of Putnam than any man in the army; he is truly the Hero of the day." Speaking for the colonies, Silas Deane wrote, "Putnam's merit rung through this Continent; his fame still increases—and every day justifies the unanimous applause of the Continent."

The army was formed into three divisions with Putnam in command of the center at Cambridge, Ward on the right, and Lee on the left. Putnam's two aides were now his oldest son, Israel, and Samuel Webb. He moved his headquarters to the Inman house, which the family had now left, and the Connecticut troops camped in fields and pine woods around it. It was only a short gallop to the house to which Washington had transferred his own headquarters. It was held a great opportunity to serve under Putnam, for he was the most popular of the commanding officers. He was friendly, hearty, fond of a joke or a laugh, interested in the men around him, concerned for the welfare of his troops, and happy to stand in line with them for rations and to cook his own. The soldiers felt they understood him, and he them, where the more aloof and formal generals did not. His men welcomed him on sight even if it meant more work.

No man in the army worked harder than Putnam, which was one of the qualities Washington liked and appreciated, for it was impossible for him to be idle or allow others to be idle around him. One afternoon Washington, riding by one of the forts to check the progress, stopped to watch Putnam encouraging the men and said, "You seem to have the faculty, General Putnam, of infusing your own industrious spirit into all the workmen you employ." Then the men worked harder than ever.

On July 18th the center division of the army was drawn up on the Common and the resolutions of the Continental Congress setting forth the causes and necessity of taking up arms were read. At Putnam's signal the men shouted a loud "Amen" followed by three cheers. Cannon were fired from the fort, and the scarlet flag sent from the Connecticut Assembly was unfurled. On one side was a scroll reading "An Appeal to Heaven" and on the other the arms of Connecticut supported by the three vines of Knowledge, Liberty, and Religion. Captain James Dana was designated to receive it and warned he must not let the colors touch the ground, as that would be an ominous sign. The six-foot captain was aghast at the honor, but Putnam clapped him encouragingly on the shoulder. So Dana marched to Washington's side, was presented with the flag by an aide, and carried it three times around the inner circle of the parade amid great applause from all the soldiers.

Washington was amazed and infuriated by much he found in Cambridge, and by the burdens now beginning to be laid on him that he would carry so long. There were courts-martial of officers for cowardice at Bunker Hill or for drawing pay for more men than they had in their command. There was little discipline, as the men held themselves as good as their officers; Ward's division was lax, above all, and he often neglected to issue orders for days. The problems were unending.

But gradually the soldiers' days took on a certain order that would endure. The day began at sunrise, or when the sentry on duty could clearly see a thousand yards around him. Then would come reveille and breakfast, assembly and morning prayers, with the orders of the day from the Commander read to every regiment. There would be drill and camp detail. Arms were cleaned, cartridges made, bullets molded. Always there was work on the earthworks, and gabions, stakes set in the ground in front of the trenches with small brush woven between and the dirt thrown behind to form a breastwork, and fascines, bundles of long brush bound together that could be carried to any parapet.

The Yankee individualism showed in the huts the soldiers built for themselves, just as it showed in their clothes. Some huts were made neatly of boards; some were of sailcloth over a frame or over a branch, some were walls of brush, and others were made of turf or stone or woven withes. For entertainment there were always church services, punishments to watch, a thief or a deserter being flogged, extra money to be made by turning any skill to good account, and games and shooting matches. Most of the soldiers, laboring with bad quills and thick ink, with words spelled as they sounded, conscientiously wrote letters home and kept diaries. Retreat was at sunset and tattoo at eight. Many of these civilians turned soldier were serious and dedicated, some were lighthearted and liked their jokes, and some were both, Putnam among them.

Once he asked for volunteers, a captain and some men from each company, for a secret and hazardous undertaking. The companies paraded. He reviewed them, complimented them on their soldierly appearance, accepted the volunteers, and dismissed the others. He then ordered them to stack their arms and equipment, take a supply of axes waiting nearby, enter a neighboring swamp, cut boughs for fascines, and bring them out on their shoulders. In the swamp the soldiers found there was a very real hazard from the swarms of mosquitoes. But through their bites they had to admit the General's description of the undertaking had been correct.

In August the men with the long rifles from Pennsylvania and Virginia arrived. In September, 10 New England musket companies, one rifle company from Virginia, and two from Pennsylvania, under Daniel Morgan, went off with Colonel Benedict Arnold on the hardship-filled and heartbreaking expedition through the Maine wilderness to meet General Richard Montgomery at Quebec and conquer Canada. Washington was trying to put the army in shape and, agreeing with Putnam that the soldiers were only as good as their officers, was cashiering some and encouraging others to retire. Nathanael Greene of Rhode Island, a Quaker who turned himself by reading books into the foremost military strategist of the army, brought in the best-disciplined troops of the camp. Henry Knox, who had been a bookseller in Boston and became the commander of the artillery, joined the army. Food was low in besieged Boston, and when Putnam heard that salt pork and fish were all that was available for the sick and wounded he sent supplies to British officers, such as Major Moncrieffe, and to American prisoners, of mutton, beef, and fresh butter. At Small's request he met the Major between the lines so the Major could thank him for saving his life. Not yet did a majority of the colonists believe there would be a revolution that would separate them permanently from England, but Putnam believed Britain would persist in her demands.

Usually other motives than gratitude prompted meetings and communications between the beleaguered city and the lines on the surrounding hills. Each side sent spies into the other camp or already had partisans who risked, if not yet life, at least jail or tar and feathering to discover the strength and intentions of the enemy. Dr. Warren himself had been in the city just a few days before his death. One of General Gage's men, disguised as a farmer, made his way to Cambridge on a Sunday morning and counted the troops as they knelt in prayer on the green after the sermon, then strolled back through Dorchester, counting men as he went. Washington established spies of his own, many of whom were never known. Others smuggled out Paul Revere's engraving tools so he could start to print money for Massachusetts and Congress. Even before Lexington and Concord, Gage was kept up to date on the deliberations of the Provincial Congress, where stores were kept, and what troops were arriving or leaving.

In September a young woman, name unknown, journeyed from Boston to Newport, Rhode Island, tried to deliver a letter to a Captain of a British ship, and failing, left it with an old friend, a baker in town. The baker forgot about it. Some weeks later she wrote and asked about the letter. After a week or so of thought, the baker took both letters to a friend of Nathanael Greene, who advised him to take them to Cambridge. He did. Greene took the man and his letters to Washington, and one was found to be in cipher. Since the baker could describe the young woman, Washington ordered her found and brought to him. Some said that through Greene, Putnam was drawn into the affair, and discovered her. Always one for prompt action, he hoisted her on the back of his horse and galloped, with her clinging, terrified, to his belt, to headquarters and dragged her up the stairs to Washington.

That General had not been a magistrate in Virginia for nothing. After several hours of questioning, she admitted the man from whom she had the letter for the Britisher was Dr. Benjamin Church, the Surgeon General and long a member of the Committee of Public Safety. A wealthy, urbane man and a good doctor, Church was popular with all and had even been on the committee that had welcomed Washington at Springfield. A chaplain and a captain of militia worked on the cipher separately; each broke the code and brought in the same translation. The letter gave Gage too much information about troops to leave any doubt—Dr. Church was a traitor and had for a long time been a spy for the British. He was arrested and tried, and though he defended himself ably was found guilty. But then it was found there was no provision for treachery in the American military code, so he was sent to Connecticut to prison, to save him from lynching. Six years later he was exiled to the West Indies and lost at sea.

Washington never forgot the Church incident (he was to build up and maintain his own very effective spy system throughout the war) nor, according to Daniel Putnam, a certain toast.

"The military family of the Commander and that of General Putnam were on most friendly terms and dined with each other once or twice a week. One day in September General Washington, at his table, gave for a toast 'A speedy and honorable peace'. All joined with apparent good will, for there was still no thought of independence.

"Not long after, at Putnam's headquarters, he rose for the toast. 'Your Excellency, the other day you gave us a speedy and honorable peace, and I, as in duty bound, drank it. Now, I hope, Sir, you will not think it an act of insubordination if I ask you to drink one of rather a different character. I will give you, Sir, "A long and moderate war." It has been truly said of Washington that he seldom smiled and almost never laughed, but the sober and sententious manner in which Putnam delivered his sentiment and its seeming contradiction to all his practice, came so unexpectedly on Washington that he did laugh more heartily than I ever remember to have seen him before or after. But presently he said, 'You are the last man, General Putnam, from whom I should have expected such a toast, you who are all the time urging vigorous measures, to plead now for a long and what is still more extraordinary, a moderate war, seems strange indeed.'

"Putnam replied, 'The measures I advise are calculated to prevent, not hasten, a peace which would be only a rotten thing and last no longer than it divided us. I expect nothing but a long war, and I would have it a moderate one that we may hold out till the mother country becomes willing to cast us off forever.' Washington, for years after and more than once, reminded the General of this toast."

Toasts, and meals, became somewhat more formal when the generals' ladies arrived in Cambridge for visits with their husbands. The wives exchanged calls and invitations—dinner was at two in the afternoon—and both friendships and a social life for the officers developed in the pleasant village.

With officers from other sections came other customs. It was a period when sometimes men, and officers, were sensitive about what they felt was their worth in the eyes of their fellows and their "honor" and believed they must prove themselves, or avenge any slight, real or imagined, on the duelling ground. Modest and tolerant, Putnam seldom encountered an affronted officer, but when he did his sense of humor took care of the problem in his own way.

Once a brother officer decided Putnam was not valuing him and his abilities sufficiently, and he accused Putnam of a hostile attitude. Growing more incensed the more he thought of his imagined wrongs, the officer demanded satisfaction on the field of honor, and immediately.

"No, no," Putnam protested. "Our services belong to our country. It would be unpatriotic at such a time for us to jeopardize the lives of two officers in such a manner unnecessarily when we are both engaged in fighting a common enemy."

But the officer became more heated and determined that a duel should take place immediately.

"Very well," Putnam agreed. "We will meet according to custom at daylight tomorrow morning."

"We will not need seconds," declared the officer.

The next morning Putnam arrived at the duelling ground the first. He was carrying an old musket loaded with slugs. The challenger soon appeared, armed with a sword and two pistols, and marched toward the General. When he was within thirty yards Putnam fired, spraying the ground around the man with slugs.

"What are you doing, sir?" cried out the officer, halting quickly. "Is this the proper conduct of an American officer and a gentleman of honor?"

"What am I doing?" Putnam asked coldly. "Why, I am defending my life against a man who wants to murder me. And if you don't beat a retreat in less time than it takes old Heath to hang a Tory you are a gone dog."

"But, sir, I . . ." began the officer, while Putnam reloaded the musket with more slugs.

Bang! Putnam's musket again sent slugs in all directions. Furious and astonished, the officer retreated, turned, and ran frantically. But later he laughed with the resourceful Putnam and became a firm friend.

The problem of housing the army, of providing shelter and rations and wood for the open fires for both cooking and heat, occupied all of the generals for most of the winter. Along with all other supplies, ammunition, and particularly cannonballs, were always short. After a fort had been built on Cobble Hill, called "Putnam's Impregnable Fortress," although it was said that any fort defended by Putnam might be considered impregnable, for it was defended with daring, courage, and intrepidity, Putnam became more eager than ever to drive the English from Boston. But cannonballs would be needed. So, one day, he ordered parties of his men, in groups of two or three, to show themselves at the top of a sandy hill in sight of the ship *Somerset,* but at a safe distance, in the hope the captain would be fool enough to fire at them. He was. So heavy a fire followed from this ship when the men were sighted and then from others nearby that many thought Boston was being attacked. Later several hundred cannonballs were easily taken out of the sand, and the fort was then well stocked. Later, other bombardments kept furnishing cannonballs.

But for one such weapon there was little ammunition. When the English brig *Nancy* was captured by the armed schooner *Lee,* and the contents were taken to Cambridge, it was found that she had most valuable stores of flints, powder, cannon, and ammunition. One object, brought overland with a good deal of difficulty, was a 13-inch brass mortar weighing 3,000 pounds. It was huge and handsome, and there was a celebration for the army when it was set up on Cambridge Common. A christening was declared in order. General Thomas Mifflin was the godfather who would give the mortar a name. General Putnam, a bottle of rum in one hand, sat astride the mortar. As Mifflin roared the name "Congress," Putnam smashed the bottle on the barrel. In spite of the loss of the rum, the troops cheered and huzzaed. It mattered little that the mortar blew up the third time it was fired.

It exploded in another celebration, for there was little

active fighting on either side, when news came that General Gage was recalled to England and General Howe was to be the new commander-in-chief. But because there was no fighting, the sense of urgency and importance dwindled among the soldiers, and those whose enlistment had expired returned home. Militia came in from New Hampshire and Massachusetts. Henry Knox, now a colonel of artillery, set off for Lake Champlain to move the cannon from the captured fortresses there to Boston, for only by bombarding the city could it be forced to surrender. And word was awaited from Arnold after the heartbreaking and terrible march through the bogs and forests of the Maine wilderness, over the Height of Land, to the plains of Quebec.

In December the terms of many of the Connecticut soldiers expired, and although both Putnam and Washington exhorted, even begged, them to stay until their places were taken by other militia, whole regiments went home, to Putnam's great disillusionment and surprise. Some of the men were shamed by the scorn of their friends and families and returned, but many did not. Late in January came the report that the assault on Quebec had failed. Then word arrived that able and admirable General Montgomery had been killed, that most of the men were dead or captured, that Daniel Morgan was a prisoner, and that Arnold and a remnant were holed up in the bitter weather just outside the city walls. At this time, too, an Englishman named Thomas Paine was writing a pamphlet in Philadelphia to be called "Common Sense" that would help to make firm the Congress and the citizens in the idea of an independent nation.

Henry Knox arrived at Cambridge with 60 cannon

dragged from the Lakes, a nearly incredible feat. Colonel Gridley marked out the works to be built on Dorchester Heights—when the group was fired on, the others ran, but Putnam waited for the lame engineer who could not run. The ground was frozen too hard to dig emplacements and trenches, and young Rufus Putnam, now a colonel of engineers, surmounted that problem by having defenses made of timbers placed on top of the ground in two parallel lines with fascines in between and held in place by posts. It was hoped the British could be lured out to attack the Heights. If they could be, Putnam with 4,000 of the best soldiers would attack Boston across the Neck. During the last Council of War about this action General Putnam was continually going to the door or the window to look out and see what was happening in the street below.

At length Washington said to him with some earnestness, "Sit down, General Putnam. We must have your advice and counsel in this matter, where the responsibility for its execution is devolved upon you."

"Oh, my dear General," Putnam replied, "you plan the battle to suit yourself and I will fight it as you wish."

On the morning of March 5th, General Howe was astounded to see on Dorchester Heights a formidable fortress with cannon mounted. "The American force has done more in one night than my whole army could have accomplished in a month," he observed sourly. It was a repetition of what he had seen in June on Breed's Hill. He was never to forget the battle on the Charlestown peninsula and the effect of the mass fire of the Americans on the advancing British lines, and ever after he was reluctant to make a frontal attack. But the guns at Dorchester must be silenced. He ordered Earl Percy with 2,400 men to embark and attack. The troops were massed, when a hurricane bore up from the south and lasted for several days. The stretch of water to the south could not be crossed, and the guns in Boston could not reach to the Heights.

So, on March 17th, Howe began to evacuate Boston, moving his army, the Tory families and their possessions, and a lot of Whig possessions also, out in his fleet. General Ward and 500 men who had had smallpox (for there were cases in the city) marched through the gate of the barricade on Boston Neck behind a flag that carried 13 stripes. Putnam and his men began landing from boats. There had been a good deal of looting, by both soldiers and civilians, Putnam discovered, but also Howe had left behind invaluable stores such as blankets and shoes and small arms. Putnam took possession of them all in the name of the United Colonies. On the 18th Washington entered Boston and requested a sermon of thanksgiving and not of war.

Chapter Nine

To Defend New York

Your long service and experience will, better than my particular directions at this instance, point out to you the works most proper to be first raised; and your perseverance, activity and zeal will lead you, without my recommending it, to exert every nerve to disappoint the enemy's designs.

Devoutly praying that the Power who has hitherto sustained the American arms may continue to bless them with divine protection, I bid you Farewell.

Given at Headquarters, in Cambridge, this

29th of March, 1776

G. Washington

So ended General Putnam's orders to proceed to New York two weeks after the British left Boston. The fleet had vanished. New York was a larger city, could draw on wider areas for food for troops, and it was so located that campaigns could be carried out in many directions. It was only a question of time before the British would appear before Manhattan.

Manhattan, an island because of the small Harlem River on the northern boundary, 13 miles from the tip, was a rocky strip of land between the wide and tidal river named the Hudson for the Englishman who found it and the narrow, turbulent strip of island-clogged water that rounds the western end of Long Island from the Sound on the north to the ocean on the south. Across a wide bay from the tip lay Staten Island, close to the curving shore of New Jersey. Because of several coves on the eastern shore, the width of Manhattan island varied between one and a half and two and a half miles. Across the Hudson the river shore in New Jersey is first lined with wide cattail-filled marshes and then farther up, with abrupt steep, straight cliffs, while the river itself presents 130 miles of wide straight waterway north to Albany. Long Island, sandy except for the heights facing part of southern Manhattan, alternately hilly and flat, is a long and fertile island itself, running east and west for over 100 miles.

The town of New York, about a mile square, lay at the lower end of Manhattan. Beyond the town the island was hilly, full of sudden outcroppings of bare rock, thick woods and brush, small ponds and brooks, but also with fields, gardens, and orchards around the handsome country homes of the wealthy. Tree-lined Broadway slanted north for two miles and then divided, the right or east fork, curving around woods and hills, continuing north to become the Post Road to Boston. The left or west fork angled toward the Hudson and then led north to end before the steeper heights below the Harlem River. More than half of the 17,000 inhabitants had been Tories, and would be again. As only brothers can hate, the Whigs and the Tories hated each other.

General Putnam arrived on the evening of April 4th. Since the city was known to be full of spies and secret enemies, security was of the first importance, though no precautions could really make the place secure. He ordered a curfew, stopped people of the town rowing out to visit the English ships still in the harbor, and continued, as Washington had directed, the various forts and fortifications begun by General Lee and General Stirling. He wrote almost daily to the Commander-in-Chief, to John Hancock, President of Congress, to the New York Committee of Safety, on all questions of public interest, and called for more men and more supplies. "Nothing was too minute for his vigilance, nothing too difficult for his industry and zeal." When Washington appeared, ten days later, he heartily approved of all that was being done.

Each day, as soon as early morning prayers at the Grand Battery were over, Putnam was everywhere, from overseeing the work on the forts, to designing the barricades being built to block the streets in case of need, to stopping a near riot single-handedly. In the evenings he was ready for a lively supper with other officers and an hour or two of talk or singing (he and his songs were always in demand), and he enjoyed the formal banquet given by the Provincial Congress of New York as much as anyone.

Late in June, Major Aaron Burr, at the request of John Hancock, became Putnam's aide-de-camp, replacing Samuel Webb, who moved to Washington's staff. Burr, now twenty-one, was of medium height, slender, handsome, a little of a dandy, with large, magnificent dark eyes which he might have inherited from his grandfather, Jonathan Edwards, the most famous of New England divines and philosophers. Burr's father had been President of the College of New Jersey at Princeton. This rather dapper young man had been a volunteer with Arnold on the expedition to Quebec, had helped tow bateaux up freezing rivers, chewed moccasins when there was no food, fought as courageously as any in the hopeless attack on the city, and earned commendations for gallantry. Burr became devoted to his "good general" and to Mrs. Putnam and the daughters who came down to keep house for the staff in the handsome Kennedy mansion at Number One Broadway, facing Bowling Green.

At the end of June the Hickey plot exploded. Thomas Hickey, one of Washington's guards, had been bribed by the British and had bribed others in turn. Arrested on the minor charge of passing counterfeit money, he had boasted in jail of his importance to Tory plots and been overheard by a prisoner who was buying his own freedom with information about others. Hickey was immediately jailed separately. A waiter in a tavern was found who had also overheard Hickey's boasts. A large Tory band was to have abducted General Washington, and though the British wanted him alive for trial, in all probability he would have been killed in the process. Every general and most of the officers were to have been assassinated and the American guns spiked so the British could take the city without a fight. Two days after Hickey was tried, condemned, and hanged, 100 British ships, men-of-war and transports, anchored in New York bay and began landing men on Staten Island. The two Howes, Admiral Richard and General William, had arrived.

It had been their hope that the display of force and might would be so formidable that the Americans, civilian and military, in New York would be terrified into accepting an offer of reconciliation with England—if the rebel armies disbanded. But it was too late for any negotiation. On July 4th the Continental Congress in Philadelphia approved the publication of the unanimously adopted Declaration of Independence, which made the thirteen colonies a nation—if they could defeat England. On July 9th the Declaration was read to the assembled troops in New York. The soldiers cheered, and then helped pull down a statue of George III that became, in part, bullets for the army.

While Washington continued his endless task of trying to build an army, and while disease and lack of sanitation and medical knowledge were already beginning to kill more men than bullets, as they would for the rest of the war, General Putnam was occupied with two plans for the confusion of the enemy. One was an effort to destroy two British ships that, ignoring the shots from the forts on both banks, had sailed up the Hudson River and anchored above the town. It was the hope of an enthusiastic group of officers that fire ships, small ships loaded with tar and combustibles set burning, could be sent down river on the two and so set them on fire. But the wind changed and the burning ships sank, and when ready the two British ships sailed serenely down the river again.

The other effort was to destroy the enemy fleet by an infernal machine. A Connecticut man, young David Bushnell, just out of Yale, had an invention that, if it worked, would destroy the British shipping. It was a one-man submarine called "The American Turtle." It was round, like a clam, and high enough for a man to stand upright. A metal doorplate on top was on hinges. It had six small round glasses, watertight, for light, and was steered by a tiller set in a waterproof joint. The man inside could sit on the floor and row with one hand and steer with the other. The rowing was hard work, for the two small oars were set like the arms of a windmill and worked by a crank. Seven hundred pounds of lead were fixed on the bottom for ballast, and the contrivance could be lowered in the water by taking in water into a tank near the bottom and raised by letting it out. There was also a glass tube with a cork and a piece of wood at top and bottom to tell how far the Turtle had descended in the water. A sharp screw on the top of the machine was intended to enter the hull of a ship, under water, and hold a magazine of powder and a clock and a means of firing the powder when the clock ran down so as to give the Turtle time to escape before the powder exploded.

Unfortunately David Bushnell was too frail to do all the work involved in managing the Turtle, and his brother, whom he had trained, was too ill. So a volunteer, Sergeant Ezra Lee, took over, and after a thorough explanation, entered the submarine. The Turtle was towed as near the British fleet off Staten Island as possible. He submerged, advanced, and found the screw was not strong enough to enter the copper sheeting of the hull. He tried again and failed, and decided to retreat to Governor's Island, as daylight was approaching. But when he passed the fort on Staten Island he could be seen moving, and a barge came out to seize whatever might be bobbing there on the dark water. Lee released the powder magazine, hoping it would blow up the barge, but at the sight of two unknown objects the barge retreated to shore.

General Putnam and a group of officers had been

watching from Manhattan and now sent a whaleboat out to tow the Turtle to safety. The magazine drifted past Staten Island and blew up in a tremendous explosion with geysers of water, all of which greatly surprised and mystified the British, for there was no sign where the explosion had come from. Amusement at the sight of the British racing to investigate and at the shouts of consternation was the only reward for the sponsors. Though it was agreed that in principle the Turtle would work perfectly, to the disappointment of all involved, the one-man submarine was never tried again.

By midsummer another fleet arrived, this time bringing the Hessian soldiers whom George III had hired to fight in America. Howe now had about 31,000 men.

Among the first troops to be settled on Staten Island was Major James Moncrieff, an old friend of Putnam's since the days when they had scouted together on the shores of Lake George. The Major had a daughter, Margaret, a witty, beautiful girl who appeared and acted much older than her 14 years. The Major wrote his friend and asked that his daughter be passed through the American lines to rejoin him. But he omitted the title of "General" on his letter, as all British officers held all Americans rebels and without real commissions. Margaret, afraid this would offend Putnam, wrote herself and asked him to overlook this omission. Putnam not only overlooked it, but arranged for her to come from New Jersey to New York and to stay with Mrs. Putnam. Margaret told all about it later.

She was introduced to General and Mrs. Washington, as the two staffs dined often with each other. Her favorite occupation was to go to the top of the big house on

Broadway and look across the Green to Staten Island through a telescope, but she was seldom allowed time alone. She found spinning flax for shirts for the soldiers with the Putnam girls boring, but she loved and admired the General and perhaps his handsome and lively aide, Aaron Burr.

One day at dinner with the Washingtons a toast was proposed, "To the Continental Congress." Margaret did not raise her glass. Instead, when that was drunk, she lifted her glass and said clearly, "To General Howe." Washington looked somewhat taken aback. Putnam hastily apologized for her on the grounds of her youth and lack of intention to offend. Washington's face cleared, and he smiled and said, "Very well, Miss, you are forgiven on the condition that when first you dine with General Howe you propose a toast either to General Putnam or to me." Gaily Margaret promised.

On August 7th Margaret was rowed in a barge to a ship near Staten Island and taken to British headquarters. That very day she was invited to dine with Sir William Howe. She found some fifty people watching her inquisitively because of her youth and her recent captivity. But she was sitting next to Mrs. Montresor, wife of the engineer, who was another old friend of Putnam's, and this gave Margaret a little confidence. Mrs. Montresor began to chat immediately to put the girl at her ease. Inevitably the toasts were begun, and inevitably she was asked to propose one.

"General Putnam," she said in a quavering voice.

"You must not give him here," a colonel rebuked her.

"Oh, by all means," Sir William broke in. "If he is the lady's sweetheart I can have no objection to drinking his health."

Blushing, and to turn the attention of the company away from herself, Margaret handed Sir William a letter from General Putnam that was to go to Major Moncrieff. It said the General was making him a present of a fine daughter, but if he did not like her to send her back and Putnam would provide her with a good Whig husband. The sentiment and the spelling amused the company, and as the wine was passed again and fans waved and the hot weather was discussed, Margaret was forgotten.

It was one of the hottest summers New Yorkers remembered. Through it all, the Americans labored on the defenses and wondered where the British would strike.

They would have their choice, for the shores of Long Island and Manhattan had too many coves and beaches for the Americans to guard or even patrol to watch for landings. And that they could land where they wished had been shown by the two ships on the Hudson.

But Washington was determined to defend Manhattan. Also, the Continental Congress wished the city held: it was the second largest in the country and strategically placed, even though half Tory in sentiment. The defense, however, meant that Washington would have to divide his army between Manhattan and Long Island. Even with experienced troops this would be unwise. With the untrained volunteers and militia, and the two portions of the army separated by the uncertain waters of the tide-harassed East River, it would be dangerous. Putnam had built a fort on Governor's Island below that river, which should hold back British ships trying to go up or down, and all along the east shore of Manhattan redoubts and barricades were available for every street. But New York could be shelled from Brooklyn Heights, and if the British held all of the western end of Long Island no tide-rip would keep them cooped up for long. So, if possible, Long Island should be held also.

There General Nathanael Greene and Colonel Rufus Putnam had planned well for the protection of Brooklyn Heights. The lines began back of the Gowanus Creek and marsh on the south, and ran northeast and then east through thick woods and placid Dutch farms and across the south edge of a low, forested ridge, above flat lands, that extended almost to the eastern end of the island. The trees and thickets on the ridge were so thick that they appeared to be almost a solid barrier. But there were several passes through this barrier that needed guarding, places where a few could hold back many. One was on the Gowanus Road, from the Narrows to Flushing; another was the Flatbush road one and a half miles from the forts, east of Brooklyn itself; still farther east was the third, on the road from Bedford to Flatbush. And four miles east was the Jamaica pass, well beyond the extreme left of the American position. So the American army extended from an indefinite spot some ten miles east of Brooklyn, around those Heights, around the rim of Manhattan Island, and up to Kings Bridge above the Harlem River. By no means could this army be drawn together except by crossing some water, and the British were in control of the waters.

Sir William Howe was in no hurry to show his mastery of seas and shoreline. For a number of days he had been trying to negotiate with Washington about a reconciliation (with each side glad to stall for time for more troops to arrive), though the Declaration of Independence had made that practically impossible. More ships and troops arrived, and more militia came in to New York. But on the morning of August 22nd, with a precision as beautiful as it was ominous, 15,000 British troops crossed the Narrows from Staten Island to Gravesend Bay on Long Island and camped on the plain. They were followed by 5,000 Hessians and Germans.

Were these to be used for the major attack on Long Island and then New York? Or would Howe use the remaining third of his army to attack New York while American eyes and arms and men were engaged on Long Island? Washington could not guess. But he knew that wherever they landed and fought, the British would have a great hidden asset—the Tories would come in with information that would be vital—where snipers were concealed, where the best roads lay, what houses had livestock and grain, who could be trusted, which important rebels should be seized or burned out. All through the war, the Tories of Long Island were of such special assistance to the British that they were practically an extra arm of the forces.

The soldiers coming to join Washington were no longer just from New England: Pennsylvania, Delaware, Maryland, Virginia, all sent regiments, and one Delaware outfit had uniforms. In all there were about 23,000 American troops, though how many were in fit condition to fight at any one time, because of illness and desertions, no one could accurately guess.

Among those laid low by bad food or bad water or fever was General Nathanael Greene, and in two days it was obvious he could not command his division on Long Island. General Sullivan, an unlucky and over-confident Irishman from New Hampshire, had been his second in command. To Putnam's delight, for he had been obviously unhappy at missing a fight, as he would if he had to stay on Manhattan, Washington gave him over-all command, with Sullivan in charge of the troops to the east and General William Alexander of New Jersey (Lord Stirling because of his claim to a Scottish title) in charge of the southern segment. Sullivan had expected to command the division in Greene's place, and Washington, choosing Putnam because of his experience and because he had been on the island, asked him to deal gently with Sullivan so his feelings would not be hurt.

On August 24th Putnam, accompanied by Burr, went to Brooklyn Heights and made an inspection of the chain of defenses there, five forts connected by entrenchments from back of the Gowanus marsh to Wallabout Bay on the north, where a third of the army was now stationed. Everywhere he moved he was greeted with cheers. Since Sullivan had charge of the eastern dispositions, Putnam did not move along the ridge or make any changes in the arrangements for the defense of the roads or for the outposts. On the 25th, Washington sent him written instructions on several points: skirmishers at outposts were to stop random firing; special precautions must be taken in the wood between Red Hook and Gowanus Creek; the militia were to be kept on interior lines.

On the 26th, Washington crossed to Long Island again and spent the day examining the defenses and by dusk knew the ground and arrangements as well as any of the generals. In the evening, with Putnam, Sullivan, and others, he rode down to the outposts near the settlement called Flatbush and went over the positions of the troops. Putnam and Sullivan later visited the pickets, and the commanders of the two most eastern companies, Miles of Pennsylvania halfway between the Bedford and the Jamaica passes, and Brodhead, also of Pennsylvania, close by, to ask if they had any clue of the British intentions. Neither officer had anything to report. Putnam, mindful of the admonition to spare Sullivan's feelings, questioned nothing he had done. Washington was sending over yet more regiments, particularly Maryland and Delaware companies for Stirling's position southeast of the Heights. To patrol effectively the lines on the wooded ridge and beyond, cavalry would have been essential, but Washington had sent back to Connecticut the only troop to volunteer, because there was not enough fodder for the horses, and the riders would not serve as infantry.

On the evening of the 26th, however, General Sullivan sent out five young militia officers, two of them recent students at King's College, to patrol the Jamaica road near Howard's tavern and the Jamaica pass. At any sight or sound of the enemy they were to carry word—and of course at least one of the five would get through—on the Bedford road, which ran back of and parallel to the long ridge, to General Sullivan so that he and Putnam would have ample warning of any British advance in that area. This was the only provision made for guarding the Jamaica pass, for none of the generals, Washington included, believed there would be any attack so far to the east when there were three other passes more convenient and accessible. But they did not give the Tories sufficient credit.

Chapter Ten

When the Americans Ran—
and the British

AT 1 O'CLOCK IN THE MORNING of August 27th, word
was brought to General Putnam that outposts near the
Narrows Road had been surprised by the enemy. Putnam
raced to Lord Stirling and ordered him to take out two
regiments. Stirling chose the Delaware Continentals, in
blue and red uniforms, under Colonel Haslet, and the
brown-smocked Marylanders under Colonel Smallwood.
By dawn they were south and east of the Gowanus marsh.
They found the enemy marching toward Brooklyn, fell
back a little, and stood firm. For several hours there was
cannonading and skirmishing, but no attack. To the east
along the ridge were two more American regiments, then
three on the Flatbush pass and two more a mile farther
on the Bedford, and farther to the east, the regiment
under Captain Miles.

Even by 8 in the morning no real attack had been reported. The only enemy in sight were the bearskin-topped

grenadiers and the Black Watch, under General Grant, in front of Stirling. At 8:30 Sullivan rode from Brooklyn to the Flatbush pass to get the latest information, and at nine it was still quiet.

It had been very quiet at 2 in the morning in the dim blackness of the Jamaica pass. Three columns of British regulars under Lord Howe, Lord Percy, and Generals Clinton and Cornwallis, had marched north from the plain and then east. Tories had told them of the Jamaica pass, where no troops were stationed. The advance guard had arrived, and, coming from behind, had scooped up the five young officers before they knew what had happened. Not one had escaped to ride to Sullivan, who had never dreamed that all five would be captured at once. Clinton had interrogated the five, and before they grew angry at his insults and refused to answer more questions, he had learned that there were no more troops for a mile or more to the west.

So, at 9:30, the British were pushing westward down the Bedford road, behind the wooded ridge and behind the American regiments on guard at the passes. The British were waiting for the bombardment to halt and the attention of the Americans to be diverted to Grant's attack.

In the meantime, Colonel Miles, suddenly concerned about the Jamaica pass, marched his company east through the woods on the ridge. Though Howe's men had been marching west on the road behind, neither had seen the other until Miles found himself suddenly confronted by an army of redcoats. A few of his men escaped and ran to warn the lines. But the first that Sullivan's men at the passes knew of danger was firing in their rear from the advancing Light Brigade. Nothing is more frightening than an enemy in the rear. Howe had executed efficiently and expeditiously a flanking movement that would become a classic, and now was preparing to roll back the American troops onto their own lines before Brooklyn, where they were to be met by the Hessians and Grant's troops coming up from the plains. More than a third of Washington's army was to be annihilated.

Experienced and inexperienced, the Continentals and militia broke and ran. By 10 o'clock in the morning, 2,000 men and officers were hurrying through the woods, up and down hills, across fields, throwing away guns and knapsacks in their frantic haste, singly and in groups, running toward the safety of the Brooklyn fortifications. Occasionally some would gather and turn to fight, but always they were driven back by numbers and bayonets, through woods and thickets, over fields and stone walls. The center broke as had the left. Riflemen who could not load quickly enough were skewered on bayonets, as were soldiers holding up their arms in surrender.

On the right behind the marsh, Stirling and his men stood firm against cannon and the charges of the regulars. But about 11 o'clock the firing on the left showed the British troops were almost in the rear, cutting off retreat to Brooklyn. Hessians and more regulars were marching, to music, to join Grant. Directly behind the Americans were mud, water, and reeds, allegedly impassable. Stirling ordered two of his regiments back, across the marsh, as best they could make their way. He kept 250 of the Marylanders under Major Gist. These were to hold back the British and allow the other troops to escape. With Stirling leading, five times they charged the green, blue, red-coated lines that so vastly outnumbered them. Four times they fell back and came on again. The fifth time, when more enemy appeared, they retired, separated, and tried to cross the marsh themselves. Only nine of them, with Gist, reached safety. Stirling, surrounded, surrendered. Alone the Marylanders had stopped the regulars and saved hundreds of their comrades. Sullivan, after trying vainly to break through to the American lines, had already surrendered, in a cornfield, to three Hessians. Shortly after noon the battle was over.

From the time the battle broke, Putnam had paced the line of the Brooklyn entrenchments. There was nothing he could do, nothing anyone could do. There were no experienced troops to send to hold back the red-coated army. As he paced he talked to the men. "If they come at us, boys, hold your fire. Wait till they are on us." But he must have been frantic that he could do no more. In the middle of the morning Washington came over from Manhattan in time to see Stirling's men hold, then charge the British. As he watched he exclaimed, "Good God! What brave men must I lose this day!"

The Brooklyn entrenchments lay on a hill that curved in a semicircle from shore to shore. Here there was no left for Howe to turn. By 2 o'clock in the afternoon the British were forming below. Then they were halted, and soon withdrawn to the plains. Howe then, as later, may well have remembered so vividly the slaughter at Breed's Hill that he refused to order a frontal attack on the entrenchments. Also, the East River was behind the American lines. His ships could sail up and bombard from the rear, but a strong northeast wind and a strong tide kept back the ships. Riding up and down, Washington and Putnam helped restore order to the exhausted and terrified soldiers who managed to reach safety and to steady the men who had been waiting so many hours. But Howe settled down, determined to attack in the proper fashion, by trenches that moved ever closer to the hill. Cold rain and an even stronger gale held the British ships immobile. But obviously when the storm decreased, the American position on the Heights would be untenable. In spite of this, Washington had brought over additional troops from New York.

By morning, the first of the British trenches, dug during the night, could be seen distressingly close to the American lines. It rained, the trenches flooded, powder spoiled, the men were sodden and exhausted. That afternoon Washington held a Council of War with his seven generals. Because of the division of the army and Howe's implacable approach, it was agreed to evacuate Brooklyn. But the evacuation must be secret. After dark General Glover's regiment of men from Marblehead, Massachusetts, who were sailors as well as soldiers, began ferrying the army of 10,000 through the blackness of waves and wind and rain in every kind of boat that could be found. Fortunately, after midnight a fog descended to muffle all sounds, and by daylight the entire army was safely on Manhattan Island. Washington was the last man to leave the Brooklyn dock. By his organization and care for every detail, his calmness and energy, he had saved the army and the American cause. He had every right to be proud of the success of the evacuation.

Who was responsible for the defeat on Long Island? Much has been written, intemperately, over the years by partisans of the generals involved. On Washington's shoulders must rest the ultimate responsibility, for his was the ultimate command, and on the 26th he spent all day on the Island and must have known and approved the arrangements. Putnam bore the next responsibility, for he was in active command and he did not question or alter Sullivan's disposition of troops or the lack of troops at the Jamaica pass. Sullivan should at least have placed a sizeable outpost, if not a company, there and not trusted to luck and five inexperienced young men. But Washington blamed no one but himself in any of his writings, merely saying that Sullivan's men had not been sufficiently watchful and had failed to prevent surprise. The whole original plan of trying to hold Long Island was at fault, but the American command was still inexperienced—and remained inexperienced, for a year later at Brandywine they were to be defeated by the same envelopment of their left against practically the same disposition of troops. Both times the British command executed a maneuver faultlessly and outclassed the Americans.

Two days later the garrisons of the forts at Red Hook and Governor's Island were brought in to New York. The enemy now could use the East River as he wished. New York was in more danger than ever. Washington asked Congress whether he should hold New York, or, if forced to abandon it, whether he should burn the city and so deny its shelter to the British. Congress replied that the city should not be burned, for it would undoubtedly be recovered, which meant that it should be defended as far as possible. His generals agreed with the Commander-in-Chief that it was impossible to hold the city but that they must try, even though the militia were departing by the hundreds and adequate defense was impossible. Five days later, Congress agreed to leave it to Washington whether to try to hold the town or not, and he and his council decided to evacuate the city. By wagons and boats the stores began to move northward. Families were sent away, and Mrs. Putnam and her daughters returned to Connecticut.

Now the army was reorganized into three divisions: Heath's, of 9,000 men, was moved north to hold a line from King's Bridge across the Harlem River; Putnam with 5,000 was to garrison New York; Greene's division was stretched from New York to Harlem along the East River. Putnam was to supervise the removal of stores, but because of the lack of wagons and horses it was a slow, laborious, and incomplete process.

Gradually Howe spread his troops around the western end of Long Island and occupied the small islands in the East River. Believing that the attack would be north toward Harlem, Washington shifted his headquarters to the Heights, whence he could move in any direction. On September 13th, a 40-gun warship moved into the East River, and that night five more anchored nearby, broadside, so close to the shore that the troops stationed at the cove called Kip's Bay could hear the calls of the sentinels.

Sunday, the 15th, was a fine hot day, too warm for the Americans in shallow ditches around the indentation on the shore. Behind them rose a low hill topped by the Murray mansion, a handsome new country house set amid gardens, lawns, and orchards. Just beyond, the Post Road angled up the island. The soldiers around the Bay were new and inexperienced, hungry and tired and bored by inactivity, and not happy about what seemed to them a very exposed position. They felt more exposed when at 10 o'clock in the morning flatboats, loaded with British troops and the blue-clad Hessians, put out from Long Island toward the line of ships. Just before 11, all the ships opened with a mighty bombardment of the shore such as had never been heard by the troops on either side. It went on for an hour, the shells throwing up dry earth to mingle with the smoke that spread over the land and the river. Then it ceased and the barges, with the red-and-white figures standing stiffly erect, began to move toward the land.

The roar of the bombardment carried up and down the island. Washington heard it in the north and hurried down with his aides. Putnam came galloping up from the south. They met back of Kip's Bay and ran into the American soldiers streaming away from where the Hessians and British were landing. A few had tried to stand and fire, but then they ran almost as quickly as the others. Washington, Putnam, other generals, their aides, all tried to rally the men.

"Take to the wall!" shouted Washington, pointing to the stone walls that edged the narrow road. "Take to the cornfield."

Some obeyed, for a moment, then trotted off to join the troops who were heading steadily to the north and to safety. Washington rode among them, pleading with them to halt and fight, then furiously commanding them. None obeyed, though a few looked apologetic. The red coats were in sight coming up the hill when an aide finally caught the bridle of Washington's horse and led him quickly away, also to the north.

But Putnam had remembered the 3,000 men back on the tip end of the island, and the artillery of General Knox. Somehow the troops must escape before the British spread out across the island and blocked the roads. On his white horse he turned south and galloped toward the city, the only figure hurrying in that direction. The soldiers on the road, curious and admiring, made way for him.

Fortunately, back in the city, young Major Burr had seen the barges of troops crossing the river and had realized the danger to the American forces. He knew the paths and side roads of Manhattan and began to round up the soldiers. To some, the men in the mud fort called Bunker Hill, he had to make a speech to persuade them he could save them from capture, but persuaded they were, and fell in behind him. Rejoicing at Burr's assurance that he could lead the army out of the trap, Putnam and his staff rode through the town, ordering, encouraging the men to start marching. The guns had to be spiked and left. By 4 o'clock in the oppressive afternoon heat 3,000 were moving, following Aaron Burr on the road that slanted westward to Greenwich Village, with its farms and pleasant houses, little hills and woods, and then north to Harlem Heights. No one yet knew whether the British had pushed their troops beyond the perimeter of Kip's Bay.

The British orders had been to land and secure the Bay and the adjacent land. This they had done, and they halted on the slopes of Murray Hill to await orders. Clinton, in command, also waited for further orders and more troops. Howe arrived, well pleased that the objective had been achieved with so little trouble and without a casualty, and joined Clinton at the Murray house for refreshments. Perhaps he thought all the Americans had withdrawn in panic from Manhattan. The troops could rest now. An attacking force, ferried across water, should build up its strength before testing the strength and intentions of the enemy. There was plenty of time.

But as Putnam saw it, there was no time. Only speed could save the men plodding up narrow lanes, for if the British had not yet cut across the island they most surely would soon. The line of men was long and weary, and the head was already nearly opposite Kip's Bay before the end had cleared the city itself. A long rise of ground separated it from the east, and as the road turned up along the Hudson, abrupt rocky humps, woods, and orchards would separate it even more effectively. Putnam was at his best in such a desperate situation. On his foam-flecked white horse he galloped up and down the line, encouraging here, giving a helping hand for a moment to a weary man there. "Move on, men, move on," he called, and, inspired, the soldiers managed to keep on pushing through woods and fields and lanes.

An officer of the 2nd Connecticut wrote: "I had frequent opportunities of beholding him, for the purpose of issuing orders and encouraging the troops, flying on his horse wherever his presence was most necessary. Without his extraordinary exertions the guards must have been inevitably lost and probably the entire corps cut to pieces."

The corps might have been lost in another way, for just two miles to the east the British were at last moving again. Fresh troops were marching north on the Post Road, which for almost the whole length of the island paralleled the Bloomingdale road the Americans were now following. Because of the heights and hollows and woods, neither force could glimpse the other, and neither threw out flankers to a sufficient distance to discover the enemy. Once the British did halt and send some skirmishers west. They met a few of Putnam's pickets struggling over the rough ground on the right of the column, exchanged fire and retired, because there had been too few to engage. The two columns were seen at last by the outposts at Harlem Heights. Colonel Smallwood and his Marylanders were sent by Washington to hold the British below a small steep dip in their road, called MacGowan's Pass, to enable the column on the west, and others retreating further east, to escape.

Finding that these Americans, for once that day, would not retreat, the British column turned west toward the Hudson. To the relief of all the marching men, it began to rain lightly. The British reached the Bloomingdale road when all but the rear guard, the 2nd Connecticut militia, had passed. There was a brief skirmish; the militia held the British, then retreated north. To the east the Maryland men also retreated, as ordered, and the British settled down for the night at the pass. At the Heights the exhausted men stumbled into the safety of the American camp. Though much had been lost in the way of stores, guns, and ammunition, Aaron Burr and Israel Putnam had saved one division of the American army.

The regiments who had fled from Kip's Bay and up the island were very conscious of their failings and ashamed of their cowardice. It rained during the evening, and there was a cold wind. There were no tents, no fires, no food. Lord Howe now held all of the island to the south. Even Washington almost despaired that he would ever have a fighting army.

The Americans were camped and entrenched in three lines on top of a steep and rocky tongue of land shaped like a finger along the edge of the Hudson and above the plain and marshes that bordered the Harlem River. This rocky tongue was Harlem Heights. At the foot of the cliff, a small narrow marsh widened from the Hudson toward the east. This was called the Hollow Way. On its south side rose another rocky hill covered with brush and trees, with cliffs running first east and then south. The cliffs on both sides were so steep that attacking the Heights would be worse than trying to climb Breed's Hill. What would Howe do next?

To try to learn this, a battalion of Connecticut Rangers under Captain Thomas Knowlton, Putnam's best and favorite captain, who had fought at Lake George and led his men astutely and bravely at the rail fence below Breed's Hill, went out at dawn. They made their way up the south side of the Hollow Way and moved south until they encountered two British battalions. Since they were on reconnaissance only, Knowlton took his men back in good order, down the cliff, across the open Way, and up a path on the north side. As they reached the top, the British appeared on the southern cliffs. A bugler, standing on the edge of the cliff, blew a fox-hunting call that told all who could hear that the fox had gone to earth. It was meant to be insulting, and it was. Washington and his officers could recognize that. The General made up his mind quickly. His troops needed something to give them back some confidence and spirit: they were ordered to stop digging trenches and assemble. Only action could wipe out "gone to earth."

He ordered Knowlton's battalion and three Virginia companies under Major Leitch to work around the right flank of the British and come on them from the rear, while some troops, making a lot of noise, descended to the Hollow Way and began first to fire and then to retreat a little. When they saw the troops below, the delighted British in turn moved down the hill, both sides firing but too far apart to do much damage. If the flanking party followed orders, at least two brigades of British would be caught in a cross-fire and trapped. Washington sent more regiments to the Hollow Way. But someone, just who was never known, gave the order to Knowlton's men to fire when they were still on the right flank and before they had reached the rear of the enemy. The Connecticut men fired, and some British swung to protect their flank. "Come on, boys," called Knowlton, and led the way up the cliff. The Virginians went with them. Both Knowlton and Leitch were hit in the first volley. Their captains took over and pressed forward. The Americans in the Way began to attack in earnest, and Washington sent more units to the aid of the attack on the flank. So did the British, but they were forced back and south. Then Washington sent two of the regiments who had run away from Kip's Bay.

As Washington sat on his horse watching, for once, the British retreat and his own men advance, a group of officers, Generals Putnam and Greene and Clinton, with some of his own aides, rode up with a request. Probably he smiled a trifle and said "Very well, gentlemen," for they made their way down the cliff and dashed across the Way and up to the heights beyond, to where the Continentals had stopped and formed their lines at the edge of a large buckwheat field that covered the flat top of the hill. As excited as the men at seeing the British fall back, the officers rode up and down behind the lines, shouting encouragement. Even when two three-pound cannon were dragged over from MacGowan's Pass to fire 60 rounds, the Americans held firm. Each side stood and fired point-blank at the other.

Then, about two in the afternoon, the British began to move back, step by step. An aide rode to tell Washington. More hurriedly the red coats and the green began retiring through an orchard south of the buckwheat. At a little hill they turned their backs and ran. Some Americans, shouting, started to chase them. The aide returned with orders . . . the advance was not to go beyond the field. Three regiments from the British reserve were coming up at a trot. The pursuing Continentals obeyed, gave one "Hurrah," and returned to their own camp on Harlem Heights.

Now the atmosphere there was very different. The men discussed what they had seen, bragged about what they had done, and exulted in describing to those who had not been there how some of the best troops of the British army had been forced to run to the rear. Some of the confidence lost at Kip's Bay and on Long Island returned. Also a ration of meat was issued. Some of the men had had nothing to eat for two days, and this cheered them further. Though they could not know it, their success made Howe more cautious than ever about joining battle and reassured Washington about the potentialities of his army. About a hundred men had been lost, but the great loss was the death of those excellent and popular officers, Knowlton and Leitch.

Howe obviously had no intention of storming Harlem Heights. His men sat down in front while he decided to go around by water and attack Washington from the rear.

During the following week New York City caught on fire—it was never discovered who was responsible—and burned for two days until the British put it out. Enough of the city was saved to give the occupying troops and officers comfortable winter quarters, but both Tory and Whig families suffered great hardship by being dispossessed from their homes throughout the winter. Generals Stirling and Sullivan were exchanged. Later, General Charles Lee returned from South Carolina. Slowly and laboriously because of lack of transport, Washington withdrew his army, reorganized into seven divisions, northward, leaving only Fort Washington on a high and craggy hill at the edge of the Hudson still in American hands.

Howe also moved slowly. On October 18th he tried to land men from barges at Throgs Neck, was discouraged, shifted to Pell's Point, and began to march inland. But the march was delayed by Colonel Glover and his Marblehead regiments (the same who had ferried the army from Brooklyn) firing from behind stone walls, with each line leapfrogging to the rear and the next wall. Washington withdrew his army to behind the village of White Plains. The British refused the battle Washington offered and attacked, on two flanks, a hill that was being entrenched. There the militia fled; the regulars retreated slowly. Putnam, sent with a regiment to help, could only hold back the British, again from behind the stone walls of farms, long enough to give the regulars time to escape. Washington withdrew again to an impregnable position at North Castle. The British returned to Manhattan: they would either attack Fort Washington or cross into New Jersey. Putnam with about 3,000 men was sent across the river.

General Nathanael Greene was in command of Fort Washington and the smaller Fort Lee on the opposite bank of the Hudson. Fort Washington was open earthworks with bastions and ample stores. Greene was convinced it could hold against a British assault of twice the garrison of 2,000 or, if necessary, he was sure they could escape by boat. It was one of his few mistakes of the war. Colonel Magaw, in command, was also sure. Putnam agreed, Washington was doubtful, and Lee felt the fort should be abandoned. Since Greene was the general in command, Washington left the final decision to him. Against all sound rules of warfare, the American army, in addition to those in the fort, was now divided into four parts; 7,000 under Lee at North Castle to guard the approaches to New England; 3,000 under Heath at Peekskill to keep the British from moving up the Hudson; 2,000 under Greene at Fort Lee, and the 3,000 under Putnam in New Jersey near the Hackensack River. As in the past, and as would be true for many months to come, militia failed to arrive, or deserted, or simply went home when their time was up. No general could be sure how many men he would have at any crisis.

On November 15th Washington, with his Adjutant General Reed, rode to confer with Putnam and Greene at Hackensack. Greene was still sure the fort could be held. Howe demanded that the fort surrender and the demand was refused, though one of its evident lacks was water. Greene and Putnam were rowed across the river, and Greene was made so confident by the spirit of the men that he sent over a thousand more. On the way back they met Washington in a skiff, still disturbed about risking the needed stores and men. Again Greene reassured him.

Early the next morning, the generals crossed the river once more and reached the eastern shore just as the battle opened on the top of the cliff above their heads. A force five times the size of the garrison had been sent by Howe. Later it was learned he had had a complete plan of the fort, its strengths and its weaknesses, furnished him by a deserter. Both Putnam and Greene wished to climb to the fort and encourage the defense, but Washington would not permit them. The attack was short and fierce. The generals had to be rowed quickly from the shore to escape capture. And Fort Washington, with 3,000 soldiers and all the stores, could do nothing but surrender.

Fort Lee was also filled with stores and cannon. On the night of the 19th, Cornwallis and 4,000 troops crossed the Hudson five miles above and came down the shore so quickly that, though Greene and all the men escaped, the breakfast kettles were still bubbling when the British arrived.

From Hackensack the army moved to Newark, where it rested a week while Washington waited for Lee to comply with his request and bring his army across the Hudson. Then the Continentals moved west, followed by Cornwallis. Both armies were short of transport. The weather turned cold and rainy. It was an exhausting, slogging withdrawal, with the American soldiers barefoot and in rags, but Washington had delayed the British advance for three weeks and brought off the scanty stores that remained. There was a short skirmish on the banks of the Raritan, and the army crawled on. Some brigades, their terms of enlistment expired, marched away though the enemy was only three hours behind.

On December 8th the army crossed the Delaware River at Trenton, with Putnam in one of the last boats.

When Howe reached the river, there were no boats left to ferry his army. But he had driven the Americans from New York across New Jersey, and winter would soon put a stop to all active warfare.

Chapter Eleven

Action in New Jersey

THAT DECEMBER THERE WAS a general feeling throughout the country that the Revolution was on the point of
collapse. Sir William Howe, reluctant to shed blood and
anxious to end the rebellion with as little fighting as possible, decided to winter in New York and clear up what
pockets of resistance might remain in the spring. He sent
Cornwallis to New Jersey to brush away the rebels there
and Clinton with the fleet to winter at Newport, Rhode
Island. With Washington and his ragged army across the
Delaware, Cornwallis's mission appeared accomplished,
and he returned to New York to sail for home leave in
England.

During the three-week retreat across New Jersey,
Washington had been hopeful that the militia would
come to the army to help defend its own homes, but none
had appeared. The army had been increased briefly by the
addition of General Lee's troops, for that general, at last
moving slowly to join Washington, had been captured

one morning by a company of dragoons and whisked to
New York. General Sullivan had led the division westward, but men kept leaving an army that could not clothe,
house, or feed them. Many in the freezing weather still
wore linen, few had wool coats, fewer blankets, and many
marched on bare feet, raw rawhide soles, or feet bound
with rags. British officers were shocked at the condition
of the soldiers they captured or killed—starving and half-
clad men should not continue fighting. Many did not, for
whole companies whose enlistment time was nearly over
left without warning or even waiting for their final day.
And on January first the majority of enlistments would
expire, and no replacements were in sight.

Nevertheless, Congress wished Philadelphia to be
held. The largest city and the capital of the new nation, it
was a neat and wealthy city. The town houses were substantial, set on streets of a decorous checkerboard pat-
tern with footwalks on each side and lights for dark
nights. A good proportion of the inhabitants belonged to
the Society of Friends, did not believe in fighting, and
lived quiet, industrious lives. There were wealthy merchants with delightful country estates around the city, a
prosperous middle class, and many inquiring minds stimu-
lated by the great Dr. Franklin. The social life was gay
and civilized. With quiet pride the city looked down on
Boston, New York, and Charlestown, just as each of
those cities surveyed the others. To the west rolled fat
farmlands that, if left undisturbed, could furnish livestock
and food for city and army, if the farmers wished. More
than half the people were ardent Tories, either active and
open or secret, and now they feared the advance of the
Continental army as the remainder dreaded the possible

arrival of the British. The security of the city was important.

Washington sent Putnam to take command. The city must be readied to resist a possible attack of the British, for no one knew their intentions. The enemy within the city must be kept under control. Water communications must be kept open for supplies. Stores must be protected. Colonel Kosciusko, a Polish volunteer, began the work on the defenses. General Mifflin, of Pennsylvania, took charge of the supplies and equipment.

On December 12th, Putnam wrote Washington that all was confusion in the city, but with his men and patrols he was bringing order. The principal stores were taken away to Christian Bridge, and he ordered a 10 o'clock curfew—people found on the streets after that hour would be arrested (and were). Then the Tories spread rumors that the Continental army was intending to burn and destroy Philadelphia to keep it from the British, hoping there would be such an attempt and a panic. On the 13th, Putnam's order put a stop to that. "The General will consider every attempt to burn the city of Philadelphia as a crime of the blackest dye and will, without ceremony, punish capitally any incendiary who shall have the hardness and cruelty to attempt it."

Congress voted Washington absolute power to direct everything relative to the war for six months and then, on the advice of Putnam and Mifflin, moved to Baltimore, leaving orders, again, that the city must be held. This departure further alarmed the city and encouraged the Loyalists in their plans to take over. But they obeyed when Putnam called all men for military service and even put some of the Friends to work on the defenses. And he announced that any refusal to accept the Continental paper money at face value would be considered a criminal offence.

But in Philadelphia, on December 19th, something happened that was to have a long and lasting effect. The journalist Thomas Paine had served as a volunteer with the American army on its heartbreaking retreat across New Jersey. Inspired by the steadfastness of Washington and the courage of the men he wrote a pamphlet, "The American Crisis." Copies appeared in the bookstores and were snatched. Copies spread throughout the states. The determined were made more steadfast, the disheartened encouraged. Inspiration came from the lines that rang through men's hearts and minds. "These are the times that try men's souls. The summer soldier and the sunshine patriot will, in this crisis, shrink from the service of this country; but he that stands it *now* deserves the love and thanks of man and woman. Tyranny, like Hell, is not easily conquered. Yet we have this consolation with us, that the harder the conflict, the more glorious the triumph."

On the 24th, Colonel Joseph Reed came to tell Putnam of Washington's plan to attack the Hessians at Trenton the next night and his desire to have several companies cross the river as a diversion. Putnam agreed to send 500 men. He knew that if he himself, and any more men, left the city the Tories would rise and take over. So Colonel Cadwallader would try to cross below the city, either by boat or on the ice, and attack the troops downstream at Burlington.

Putnam must have felt bitterly disappointed that his duty would not let him take part in this secret, desperate venture. Leading the men on a silent night march, forming the lines quietly for attack, rushing the enemy wherever found, this was his kind of warfare, the kind he and the men understood. He must have wished throughout the night that he was with the 2,000 tramping the muddy freezing roads to where the men from Marblehead waited in the 50-foot Durham boats built for ferrying on the Delaware. Glover had said his troops would get the army across, and they worked the deeply laden, flat-bottomed scows through floating blocks of ice, back and forth, until the army and the cannon were landed nine miles above Trenton. Even the laborious march in cold that was so bitter two men, at a rest, froze to death would not have dismayed Putnam. He must have envied his old friend John Stark when he heard how Stark led his men with a roar through the little town to help close the trap on the bemused Hessians and then had the exhilaration of seeing these feared troops laying down their arms.

By noon the army, with the captured ammunition, field pieces, baggage, and 900 prisoners, was marching back to the Delaware, and again Glover's men, who had fought with the best, were once more carrying all to safety. The Hessian officers were sent to Philadelphia in five canvas-covered wagons to "The Indian Queen" inn and given a good supper that evening. The men, followed by the captured guns, flags, and regimental standards, were marched to the city. Putnam had them parade, with drums rolling and fifes playing, up and down through all the streets to show that the dreaded Hessians could be captured, lodged them in the barracks for a week, and sent them off to Baltimore. The officers were brought to call on the General, who shook hands and gave each a glass of Madeira.

The news of Trenton brought heart and hope to the patriots throughout the country. Some militia trickled in. The army had been considered exhausted and on the point of vanishing. Suddenly it had taken the offensive and showed it could fight and win. The Revolution was not dead, after all.

But it was on the point of expiring for lack of men to fight. In camp, Washington went from regiment to regiment, begging the men to stay another six weeks even though their terms were up. Desperately he offered, from his own pocket, ten dollars in hard money to each man who would stay that long in the army. Some decided to stay, and then more, and other generals had some success, and there was still an army that remembered Trenton.

Cadwallader and his men, not having the Marblehead men and boats at hand, had been prevented by the ice from crossing the river on the crucial night, but had succeeded two days later. Washington moved his army back again to Trenton. Cornwallis, his leave cancelled, had hurried back, gathering regiments, and now was camped across the little creek that runs through the town. Though urged to attack that evening, Cornwallis decided to wait until the next morning—he had more men and guns, and there could be no doubt about the result. Some unknown officer in Washington's Council of War suggested a retreat by back roads, unknown to the British, and an attack on their troops at Princeton, 12 miles to the northeast. Leaving behind a rear guard to tend the fires and make as much noise as possible throwing up earthworks, the army moved in silence over muddy roads suddenly and luckily made iron-hard by freezing.

At sunrise two British regiments set out from Princeton, drums beating, flags flying. They were to join Cornwallis at Trenton for the final destruction of the American army. Hoarfrost shone on the dried grass in the fields; trees and bushes glittered. Suddenly, on the left, the sun glinted on rows of muskets as Mercer's division approached at the same time the bridge over Stony Brook on the Trenton Road. The two lines, formed, fired. Seeing the encounter from a distance, Washington sent forward Cadwallader and the militia. The Redcoats charged with bayonets against Mercer's company, whose rifles took so long to load, and the men began to retreat. The militia broke and carried back the Continentals.

Washington, obviously, was not going to have another Kip's Bay debacle. Followed by one aide, on his big white horse he galloped straight between the two opposing lines. As he rode he shouted, "Follow me, men. Hold your fire." Greene and Cadwallader dashed among the militia forming them into lines. Washington was 30 yards from the red soldiers. Two volleys were fired; smoke covered the ground. The aide covered his eyes; he could not bear to look, thinking the General must have been shot. But then the smoke cleared. There was Washington, untouched, calling again to the militia. Three Continental regiments appeared, and the British halted, gave a ragged volley, and fled. That was enough for the militia. With Washington in the lead they streamed after the British. The Commander-in-Chief, all else forgotten, stood up in his stirrups and swung his hat. "Come on, boys," he shouted at the top of his lungs. "It's a fine fox chase." And he galloped after the redcoats, militia racing behind. But there was danger in following the running soldiers too far, and reluctantly he called back the pursuit and led the men on to Princeton, which was now, with some prisoners, in American hands. Putnam would have enjoyed that fox chase to the hilt.

Few Americans were lost in the battle, and not many stores were captured. But as happened so often, the real loss was in the fine officers. General Mercer, who had been with Prince Charlie at Culloden in 1745, Colonel Haslet of the Delaware regiment that had stood at the Gowanus marsh to save their comrades, Captain Fleming of Virginia, none of them would again call "Come on, boys" as they led a charge.

Although it was a temptation to try to capture New Brunswick with its stores and pay-chests, the army was exhausted from 40 hours of marching and fighting without sleep or food. Instead, Washington moved it north and east into the hills around Morristown for winter quarters.

Three days after the battle, Washington wrote to Putnam about the action, telling him that it was his hope to drive the British out of New Jersey. He moved Putnam to Crosswicks to keep watch on the enemy and then to Princeton. He was to give out his strength as being twice what it actually was and to keep as many spies in the field as he felt proper—horsemen in the dress of the country riding back and forth to discover any movement of the enemy.

The victories of Trenton and Princeton caused Howe to pull back toward New York most of the posts he had established in New Jersey, except for New Brunswick and Paulus Hook. This was fortunate for the people of the state. During December the Crown troops had ranged freely far and wide, plundering Tory and Whig households alike. Northeastern New Jersey was for the Revolution, but Newark and Elizabeth and the central counties were largely Tory in sentiment. When Washington retired from the state, rejoicing Tories began to return to their homes, trusting to the British troops to protect them, while many who had wavered between the two causes came in to take the oath of loyalty to the Crown. But to the Hessians the plunder of an occupied territory made up for what they did not receive in pay, and this was true, to a somewhat less degree, with the English soldiers. Throughout central New Jersey, Tories and Rebels alike were compelled to watch their household goods being carried away, their cattle and livestock confiscated, their food stores taken or wantonly destroyed. They soon counted themselves lucky if their homes were not burned and if they and their families were not brutally mistreated or killed. Whatever goods the plundering soldiers left, the camp followers—women, servants, drummers—carted off or scattered, until even the British officers protested to Howe that his promises of security to the people were mocked and disregarded. But after the two victories, the spirit of loyalty to the Crown flickered and fell as hope for the new nation rose throughout the country. Men and foodstuffs began to come to the army at Morristown, and Congress moved back to Philadelphia.

At every new post, Putnam made a meticulous inspection of the arrangements for the billeting of his own troops, the outposts, the cooking arrangements, the hospitals, and the comfort of the wounded. In the hospital at Princeton he found a Captain McPherson of the 17th British regiment who had been shot in the chest during the battle. Considering him a hopeless case, no surgeon had given him any care. He was still alive, however, after three weeks of neglect, though he was wasted and suffering when Putnam stopped by his pallet. He asked the Captain what had happened and the attendant why the officer had not been washed and fed and the wound probed. Annoyed at the treatment of an honorable enemy, Putnam had the officer moved to a private house and a surgeon brought to care for the wound and gave orders that he was to have the best possible treatment.

The next day he returned to the patient, who thanked him and then asked, "Pray, sir, what country man are you?"

"An American," Putnam answered with a smile.

Unable to believe this the Captain asked, "But not a Yankee, surely?"

"A full-blooded one," replied the General, proudly but laughing.

"By God, I am sorry for that," exclaimed McPherson. "I did not think there could be so much goodness and generosity in an American, or, indeed, in anybody but a Scot."

Putnam was amused, and liked the man, and often visited the prisoner as he slowly recovered. One day McPherson asked that a fellow officer be allowed to visit him from New Brunswick, so that he might see a friend and give him instructions about his own affairs in case he should not recover. At first the General was reluctant for he did not wish any of the enemy to see how small a number of men held Princeton, but he was too kind-hearted to deny the request entirely. And then he saw how he might follow one of Washington's suggestions.

He sent a messenger under a flag of truce to the British camp with private orders to the guard not to return with the officer until after dark. When they arrived, the handsome three-story building of the College of New Jersey had a candle in very window. Every house was blazing with lamps or candles or lanterns. The streets were full of soldiers, officers strolling, squads marching, soldiers moving through the town. All that evening, while the two British officers visited in a first-floor room on the main street, they could watch first a regiment pass, then an informal group of men without hats, then a quick-stepping squad in a different uniform, as Putnam maneuvered his small force down the street, around back of the houses, into different caps or coats, to march or stroll by the window again. In the early hours of the morning, and while all the lights still flickered, the friend was escorted back to New Brunswick. He reported that Putnam had at least four or five thousand active troops at Princeton (he had less than two) and certainly could not be dislodged with less than twice that number.

During those winter months in New Jersey, the British were constantly harassed by small armed groups from Princeton ambushing supply trains, capturing messengers, seizing foraging parties. Putnam's men captured a thousand prisoners. With most of them he was lenient, but where the "skinners" and "land pilots," independent bands who were dreaded for their ferocity and cruelty, were concerned he sent them in chains to jail in Philadelphia. Soon disillusioned Tories as well as loyal Whigs began to send word to Princeton or Morristown when raids were expected or a convoy was being assembled. From behind the Watchung range, Washington sent out many raiders and ordered that grain and hay were to be destroyed wherever found so that the British cavalry would not be strong enough to defend the wagon trains bringing supplies.

In March came word that French supply ships were arriving in Boston and Philadelphia with flints and fine powder as well as arms and clothes for the troops—but there would never be enough. Soldiers who had been captured at Quebec and were now exchanged were reaching camp. With spring the campaigns would open. What were the British planning, and where would they strike?

Chapter Twelve

"Who Dared to Lead Where Any Dared to Follow"

THE MYSTERY OF THE British intentions would be one of Washington's chief preoccupations for the coming years. There was no way of discovering, and the guesses of the generals and of Congress were frequently wrong. In the spring of 1777 there was a rumor that an expedition would be moving from Canada down Lake Champlain. In May, General Putnam was sent north to Peekskill to take charge of the troops on both sides of the Hudson River.

The Hudson Highlands are a group of abrupt, rounded, heavily wooded hills that lie across the river north of New York City and south of the Catskill Mountains. Two small forts, Clinton and Montgomery, seven miles below West Point, were commanded by Generals George Clinton, Governor of New York, and his brother, James Clinton. A boom of logs and iron chain was built across from Fort Montgomery to Anthony's Nose on the east bank to prevent (it was hoped) the British fleet from moving up river. The completion of this was General Putnam's responsibility.

In July, Howe withdrew his men from Staten Island, and a fleet of 200 ships disappeared over the horizon. No one knew their destination. News came of the fall of Fort Ticonderoga to General Burgoyne, who was advancing with an army south from Canada. Seven thousand men were left in New York City under Sir Henry Clinton. Also in July, Aaron Burr was made Lieutenant Colonel, at twenty-one the youngest in the Continental army, and he regretfully left Putnam's staff for a practically independent post on General Maxwell's staff in New Jersey.

The Highlands and the rest of southern New York State was a land torn and devastated by a bitter civil war of Whig against Tory. Neighbor spied on and denounced neighbor, grudges were remembered and avenged, houses and barns were burned, and as always the civilians suffered more than the troops or the armed irregular bands. Putnam was severe and stern with offenders. Deserters were hanged. On one he had posted a notice: "I wish that all who have an inclination to join our enemies from motives of fear, ambition or avarice, would take warning by this example and avoid the dreadful calamaties that will invariably follow such vile and treasonable practices."

Spies were hanged. A man in civilian clothes was caught in the American camp, with evidence that proved beyond doubt he was a spy sent by Clinton. Since the British had many spies, word quickly reached New York that this Edmund Palmer was in jail. Sir Henry wrote to Putnam that he represented no acknowledged sovereignty and so could not possess any legal authority to inflict the death penalty on the man.

Putnam replied: "The man Edmund Palmer was caught as a spy; he was tried as a spy; he was condemned as a spy; he will hang as a spy. Yours, I. Putnam. PS. He has been hung."

But he wished he did not have to punish his own troops. As he put in General Orders: "The Gen'l is sorry that he is so frequently put to the disagreeable Necessity of ordering Punishments to be inflected owing to the great Frequency of Crimes, the Perpetration of which renders punishments absolutely necessary for the Reformation of Offenders and to deter others in order to maintain the Order and Regularity which is necessary for the well-being of the Army." Though there were trials nearly every day, not all ended fatally, and many offenders received light punishment. An officer was cashiered for behaving in a cowardly manner in the presence of the enemy, and a soldier for plundering, but a sentinel found asleep was pardoned because he had been on active duty for two nights before and was asleep while standing up.

The General was always delighted when there was any excuse for a little recreation for the men, and the first anniversary of the Declaration of Independence was certainly the best of excuses. He arranged a feast with songs, fireworks, speeches and toasts, and something special. The Highlands rise steeply from the river. On top of a cliff nearby, Putnam had found an immense six-ton rock so perfectly balanced that a little force would send it down the bank into the river. When the feast was over, the troops not on duty were drawn up on the plateau with the officers in full uniform. Putnam made a lively speech and gave the order. The men on the lever heaved. The great rock fell with a tremendous crash down through the trees and bushes to the water. At the same time guns were fired and the echoes rolled and reverberated back and forth from the cliffs. As the rock went down, one party of officers shouted together, "So may the thrones of tyrants fall." When the rock disappeared in the water, another group answered, "So may the enemies of freedom sink to rise no more." All who were there said it was a most gratifying celebration.

Putnam was popular with his officers and enjoyed giving them good advice disguised as tales of his own experiences. He had no patience with the custom of duelling and had one story to show how ridiculous were the pretensions involved.

A British officer, who was a prisoner of war on parole, once took offense at something Putnam said about British officers in general and sent a letter challenging him to a duel, without seconds. Putnam accepted the challenge and pointed out he had the right to choose the weapons and place.

The officer appeared promptly and found Putnam sitting on a stool beside a large powder keg, with grains of powder scattered thickly on top of the barrel. The General saluted, then waved toward a stool on the opposite side of the keg. "Sit down there," he ordered in a voice not to be questioned.

The officer opened his mouth to object, then sat down. Putnam waved the pipe he was smoking in the air, then touched the coals to a slow match that was sticking out of a hole in the side of the keg.

"Here is my choice of weapons," Putnam told the officer. "It is perfectly fair. We both have an equal chance of being blown to bits when the keg goes up."

The Britisher looked at Putnam, at the large keg, at the burning match. The fire was moving steadily toward the hole. The officer jumped to his feet, backed away, then more and more quickly retreated.

"You're just precisely as brave as I took you to be," Putnam called after him. "But now you've left the field of honor you needn't hurry. There's nothing in the barrel but onions. I thought I'd try you on onions first. But," with a shout of laughter, "you don't like the smell, I guess."

By then the officer was out of earshot. And Putnam was still laughing.

Many of Putnam's small army were farmers, and at the thought of their fields uncut and their harvests untended, they became restless and sullen. There was no word of Howe during August. So, since some were leaving without permission, the General allowed more to go home for harvest, believing that the recruits he had requested from Connecticut would fill their places. And he and two of his generals had plans, which Washington had approved, to create a diversion of his own by attacking Staten Island and Long Island, but Washington began to call for troops to be sent south to his army.

Howe at last sailed up the Chesapeake and landed his army at the head. He knew, of course, of Burgoyne's invasion, but through carelessness in England explicit orders to sail north and meet the advancing army and cut off New England from the country were never sent to him. He did receive one letter with a general hope that he would be able to do this, which should have been enough, but perhaps he thought he could take Philadelphia and still have time to meet Burgoyne around Albany, or that Clinton would move north more quickly. Howe defeated the Americans at Brandywine and a month later at Germantown.

Not until after the fall of Philadelphia did Sir Henry Clinton start up the Hudson to create a diversion to assist Burgoyne. The boom across the river was easily passed. Shipping, houses, and mills were burned. A message was sent from Fort Montgomery to Putnam asking for more troops, but the messenger turned traitor and vanished. Although both the little forts were defended with persistence and courage, both were captured, but the commanders and many of the men escaped down the steep banks to the river. The prosperous Dutch town of Esopus was burned, and Clinton returned to New York, abandoning the forts. Though Putnam and the American Clintons worked well together, they had too few troops to prevent the raids and burnings by the British. Later they were to be blamed for the loss of the forts.

News of the surrender of Burgoyne reached General Putnam two days after it occurred. He forwarded the dispatch to Washington, and then the terms, which General Gates, who had commanded the American army at Saratoga, had not done in his eagerness to get word of his success first to Congress. In the same month Mrs. Putnam, who had come to stay with the General at Peekskill though she had not been well, died, which affected him deeply, for they had had a good life together.

The troops released from the army in the north were now moving down the Hudson, and at first word came from Gates that 5,000 would join Putnam's forces. The idea of attacking south, perhaps even New York, was revived. But a 20-year-old officer named Alexander Hamilton arrived at Putnam's headquarters and peremptorily ordered the General to send these new troops and his remaining Continentals on to General Washington, who wanted them for his own use. But Putnam, a veteran of 20 years and a Major General, was not used to being ordered rudely by a boy and was not convinced of Hamilton's authority. He wrote to inquire. When Hamilton returned from his trip to Albany, the troops had not moved. Hamilton wrote a lofty, harsh, and nearly hysterical letter ordering again the forwarding of the men.

Most of Washington's generals were extremely touchy individuals when they thought their rights, credits, privileges, and "sacred honour" were concerned. Most of them, Gates, Lee, Schuyler, Sullivan, Arnold, Wayne, Morgan, even Knox and Greene, for years kept Washington busy soothing their ruffled feelings and explaining that they had not been slighted by him, by Congress, or by others. Generous, modest, and good-natured, Putnam had ignored all provocation and never given the harassed Commander this problem. But now he was outraged by Hamilton's manner and letter. He forwarded it to Washington with one of his own saying that he felt that Hamilton's contained "some most unjust and injurious reflections" upon himself and asked for more direct orders. But Hamilton had reached Washington first and complained violently of the veteran general's failure to acknowledge his authority. Washington sent back a brief note saying that Hamilton had had authority and he could wish his requests would be honored more quickly in the future. Putnam sent the troops south immediately. He was left with a small force of militia.

The partisan warfare increased, with estates and homes of both Whigs and Tories being burned by bands from both armies and particularly by independent raiders who robbed and killed both sides. And now people of New York State began to complain about General Putnam. He became particularly unpopular with those who had the disposal of Tory property, because he was sorry for the families and tried to see justice done. Others complained he was too kind to prisoners. Some objected because he gave passports to Tories to go to New York on personal business.

He exchanged newspapers with some of his British officer friends in the city, though he advised them to have the real news in his printed instead of the falsehoods in theirs. He should not have lost the forts—though Washington and the army knew well that they were lost because they had not had enough men to defend them. Even his letters and orders were distorted and changed when reported to Washington, and Hamilton was continually undermining with complaints Washington's regard for the General. Probably Putnam did not suspect the campaign against him, for he trusted the honor and integrity of others as he trusted his own.

In mid-December he asked permission to return to his home in Connecticut briefly because of family affairs. Washington urged him first to go to the Highlands and examine the possible sites for forts. So with the two Clintons, some officers, and a French engineer, the various spots were gone over, and all except the engineer agreed that West Point was by far the best place. Since the engineer had the confidence of Congress and Washington, the matter was referred to the Council and Assembly of New York State. A committee was sent, and West Point was chosen unanimously. Putnam ordered Parsons' brigade to break ground, but the engineer was disgruntled and slow in laying out the works, and the extreme cold, the privations of the men, and the lack of teams and tools made the work advance very slowly.

Early in February Putnam reported to Washington that a new chain was being forged to go across the Hudson and also that: "Meigs regiment is at West Point and until barracks can be built it is best to keep them there. Dubois' regiment is unfit to be ordered on duty, there being not one blanket in the regiment. Very few have either a shoe or a shirt, and most of them have neither stockings, breeches nor overalls. Several companies of enlisted artificers are in the same situation and unable to work in the field. Several hundred men are rendered useless merely for want of necessary apparel as no clothing is permitted to be stopped at this post." No clothing came. Soon Putnam returned to Connecticut for two months' leave.

In February a treaty of alliance was signed with France, which Congress took until May to ratify, and now ships with supplies could sail openly for America, and the French ships could attack the British. In the same month a flag with red and white stripes and thirteen stars on a blue square in the corner was officially adopted by Congress. In March, Washington appointed General McDougall in command of the Highlands, sent Rufus Putnam and Kosciusko to fortify West Point, and in April ordered, because of the demands from New York State, a Court of Inquiry into the loss of Forts Montgomery and Clinton. General Putnam returned to Fishkill before he was told of any of these actions. But the Court agreed the loss of the forts was not through any "fault, misconduct or negligence of the commanding officers but solely through the want of adequate force under their command to maintain and defend them." Putnam and the Clintons were exonerated of all blame. Even those who did not know him realized there were more reasons than appeared for forcing the inquiry. A British officer at Philadelphia wrote:

"We hear that Mr. Putnam was lately tried before a court-martial and honorably acquitted on the charges brought against him. The principal one was leniency toward prisoners—a sentiment he seems to have imbibed years ago when he had the honour to serve His Majesty for several years in the late War."

Washington then asked Putnam to take charge of the recruiting service in Connecticut where, aided by Governor Trumbull, he quickly raised and forwarded the troops desired. In June Howe evacuated Philadelphia, sending the Tories who wished to leave and their baggage by ship to New York but, because of possible danger from the French fleet, marching his army, under Clinton, overland. Washington and his army followed and won a victory at the Battle of Monmouth Court House. The disgrace of General Lee there and the court-martial that followed made General Putnam the highest ranking general in the Continental army, next to Washington.

Clinton moved on to New York, while Washington took his army to the Hudson above the city. Now both armies were back where they had been two summers before. But the situation had changed. Washington had an army that had been well-trained and drilled by Baron von

Steuben the winter before and which could face the British veterans in any battle. The British no longer believed they could conquer the northern portion of the country and turned their attention to the southern states. Never again would there be a major military engagement between the two forces north of the Potomac.

General Putnam joined the army at White Plains in command of the "Virginia Line." One surgeon writing of his visits to the hospitals and his solicitude about the care and comforts of the patients said: "In his person he is now corpulent and a little clumsy, but carries a bold and undaunted front . . . It is famed of him that he has, in many instances, proved himself as brave as Caesar." A little later, when Putnam was in command at West Point, the same surgeon described a dinner given in honor of General Muhlenberg at which Putnam was asked to preside and "displayed no less urbanity at the head of the table than bravery at the head of his division." The banquet, for forty-one officers, had fourteen different dishes "served in fashionable style." It was followed by a number of toasts, "numerous and merry songs and in the evening we had military music and dancing."

Winter quarters for three brigades of New York and Connecticut troops were around Danbury, Connecticut, to protect vulnerable towns along Long Island Sound and yet be near enough to aid the Highlands in case the enemy should move north from New York. Washington was at Middlebrook, in New Jersey, where he could quickly reach either New York or Pennsylvania. The Connecticut camps were in the sheltered valley of the Saugatuck, with Putnam's headquarters in a farmhouse on Umpawaug Hill on the Danbury road. David Humphreys, who had been a Major with General Parsons, had served with Greene, and been on Washington's staff, was now his aide, and a deep friendship developed between the two men. Putnam's two other aides were his sons, Israel and Dan. Joel Barlow, the Connecticut poet, visited the headquarters for several weeks and while there wrote his long patriotic poem, "The Columbiad," which was greatly admired.

But the quiet and leisure of camp life allowed the troops time to consider their grievances. They had few clothes or blankets, no pay, and not much food. Just before Christmas, Huntington's brigade gathered under arms to march to Hartford and demand redress from the Legislature. When Putnam heard of this, he mounted his horse and ordered a group of drummers to follow him. He reached the regiment and with drums beating rode slowly along the line as if the men were on review. From habit they presented arms. He halted in front of them and made a speech.

"My brave lads, where are you going? Do you intend to desert your officers, and to invite the enemy to follow you into the country? Whose cause have you been fighting and suffering so long in? Is it not your own? Have you no property, no parents, wives or children? You have behaved like men so far; all the world is full of your praise, and posterity will stand astonished at your deeds, but not if you spoil all at the last. Don't you consider how much the country is distressed by war, and that your officers have not been better paid than yourselves? But we all expect better times, and that the country will do us ample justice. Let us all stand by one another, then, and fight it out like brave soldiers. Think what a shame it would be for Connecticut men to run away from their officers!"

As he finished, the soldiers gave a loud cheer and in great good humor marched to their quarters and stacked their arms. So ended that possible mutiny. Only one soldier, the one who had begun and kept alive all the trouble, was placed under arrest; he was shot by the sentry while escaping. Washington, who knew what it was to have troubles with troops, sent a warm letter of congratulation and commendation on the successful manner in which Putnam had handled the problem.

Late in February Governor Tryon, who had been Tory Governor of New York and had become a British General, set out from near King's Bridge to raid a part of Greenwich called Horseneck and destroy the salt works, which were important because salt was scarce. His advance was discovered by thirty men of Putnam's scouts. They skirmished, were attacked, retired, halted, then retired again in the direction of Horseneck.

General Putnam had been on a tour of his outposts at West Greenwich. There are several accounts of what happened at nine the next morning. One was that he was at a tavern near the hill above Horseneck; another, that he was at a house nearer the hill when the enemy approached walking their horses. But the most popular one was that he was staying with General Mead and was shaving in a front room when reflected in the mirror he saw the mass of red coats advancing from the west. Only half shaved, he seized his sword, rushed to his horse, and started for a hill a half-mile away to rally the 150 men he had with him. He stationed them on the edge of the hill by the Congregational Church, had them bring up two old field guns, and waited. The British came on in a solid column, but just out of range, deployed to right and left to flank the Americans. In the front rank were some of the most vicious and vindictive Tories, Delancey's regiment from New York. Putnam discharged the field pieces, but without enough effect. Obviously his men were greatly outnumbered. "Retire," Putnam ordered. "Form on that hill over there and hold. I am going to Stamford and will collect the militia and troops there and will return with them immediately."

He wheeled his horse into the main road. Some British dragoons left their ranks to chase him, and he put his horse to the gallop. The ring of steel from the horses' hooves on the hard ground behind told him the enemy were gaining. A quarter of a mile east the road curved north around the hill. Putnam turned his horse from the road and dashed straight toward the precipice, over the edge, and down the side. Startled, the dragoons reined back their horses. They did not dare to follow down that steep and dangerous descent. They fired, and one ball pierced his cap. Putnam waved his sword in derision and was off on the road to Stamford. As he galloped, he passed a woman carrying milk pails to her house while four little girls played near the road. "For God's sake, madam, take in your children, for the British are upon us," he shouted as he sped by.

When he returned with reinforcements, he found that his men had retreated to a distant hill, not the nearby one to which he had pointed, and the enemy had destroyed the salt works, a sloop, and some stores in Cos Cob. As they withdrew they pillaged some houses in Greenwich. But the Americans pursued, and Putnam had the satisfaction of picking up stragglers and an ammunition and baggage train of wagons piled with plunder. He enjoyed restoring the pillaged goods to their owners. Because of his kindness to the wounded prisoners, who were exchanged later, and in recognition of his bravery, Governor Tryon sent him a new suit of military clothes, with a new hat.

When spring came, the troops were sent back to the Highlands. Putnam in his farewell order praised them for their "Regular and Soldier-like Conduct" and wished them "a Successful and Glorious Campaign." Now in command of the right wing of the army, his headquarters was at Buttermilk Falls, two miles below West Point. From here he happily harassed the enemy and enjoyed the friendship of the officers of the line. General Anthony Wayne and 600 men of the Light Brigade stormed and took the British fort at Stony Point, though it had to be destroyed and abandoned; Light Horse Harry Lee attacked Paulus Hook, in New Jersey. These two actions kept the British uneasy about their outposts. In October, Clinton moved south to attack Charleston, and Washington sent most of the regiments after him. In November Putnam was given leave. On his return he would be with Washington in winter quarters.

After fourteen days at home, he set out in December to rejoin the army at Morristown, but before he reached Hartford a strange heavy sensation began to spread along his right side. When he reached the house of his friend Colonel Jeremiah Wadsworth his side was paralyzed. At first he could not believe this had happened to him, and he tried to get rid of the trouble by exercise so he could go on to the army. But the paralysis remained. In deep dejection he was forced to send word to Washington that he could no longer serve with the troops. He could do nothing but return to Pomfret and the old homestead, where now his elder son lived with his family.

Epilogue

Though General Putnam could no longer take an active part in the war, through visitors, travelers, and papers, news of it came steadily to Pomfret, and he could follow its course.

During the winter of 1780 the value of the Continental paper money fell to nothing. At Morristown, where Putnam would have been with Washington in winter quarters, for six weeks the soldiers received an eighth of the normal amount of rations. But when Clinton moved the British fleet and an army south to besiege and capture Charleston, the military action, except for some coastal raids, would thereafter be south of the Potomac. General Gates was sent by Congress, against Washington's wishes, to command the southern army. Because of his obstinacy and blunders Gates led the American army into the worst defeat of the war at Camden, South Carolina. Before the battle was over, he was galloping north to safety; he was never given another important command.

But a small army of American frontiersmen once more raised the hopes of the country by defeating and capturing an army of Tories of the same size at King's Mountain. Major Ferguson, the only British soldier in the battle, was killed. Putnam, of course, knew Benedict Arnold, the valiant soldier of the Quebec and Saratoga campaigns, and must have been astounded, with the rest of the country, at the news of the treachery Arnold had planned in delivering the fort at West Point to the British.

In 1781 Daniel Morgan, who had been ignored and passed over for promotion by Congress more often than had Arnold, came from his Virginia farm to serve under Nathanael Greene, the new commander of the southern army. By a perfectly planned battle and expert use of militia, Continentals, and cavalry, he completely defeated an equal force of British regulars under Colonel Banastre Tarleton, capturing all but a hundred, and then, pursued by Cornwallis, retreated north to North Carolina and Greene. The British were unable to follow far because of lack of supplies and boats to cross swollen rivers. Later, Greene and Cornwallis met at the Battle of Guilford Courthouse where, although Cornwallis won the field, he was so weakened he had to retreat to Wilmington to recoup. Aided by effective guerilla bands and their daring leaders, Greene won back most of South Carolina. Cornwallis marched into Virginia to establish a base for sea communication with Clinton in New York.

The war in the northern and middle states had long been one of grim endurance, with thousands of Tories joining the British forces and increasing the terrors of civil war (100,000 Tories were ultimately to leave the country), and the patriots waiting for England to tire of the struggle. A French fleet and army took Newport, Rhode Island, from the British, but were contained by a British fleet, and Washington was unable to carry out his wish to attack the British base in New York. Admiral Rochambeau brought a French fleet north. He and Washington met and planned an attack by land and sea against New York, and 5,000 French troops moved overland to join Washington's. But an attack on the British army in Virginia would be more practical, particularly if De Grasse would bring his fleet from the West Indies. He agreed, and sailed north in August with 3,000 soldiers. Washington and the allied forces began a formal siege of Cornwallis's position at Yorktown. More French ships arrived. The British fleet engaged and withdrew. On October 19th Cornwallis surrendered. His troops marched to stack their arms to the tune "The World Turned Upside Down." And so it was. To the amazement of the world, 13 disparate, unorganized, and feeble colonies had won by arms their independence from powerful England.

Peace talks were begun, then formal negotiations, and finally the peace treaty was signed in September, 1783. In December, the British completed the evacuation of New York. Washington took leave of his officers at Fraunces' Tavern in that city and at Annapolis resigned to Congress his commission of Commander-in-Chief.

The colonies were now independent states united as the Confederation of the United States, but the problems of peace were as great as those of war. New state constitutions had been adopted, but the Articles of Confederation, and Congress under them, were weak; trade declined, and government credit fell lower and lower. At last, in 1787, a Constitutional Convention opened in May at Philadelphia, a Constitution was finally drawn, and by July 1788, it had been ratified by the necessary nine states. In January, presidential electors were chosen. In April the ballots were counted, and Washington was unanimously elected President. On April 30th he took the oath of office in New York. Putnam must have rejoiced at the wisdom of the country and the honor for his commander.

All this had happened since Putnam's resignation from the army. It was hard for him to admit that his military life was finished. But by May, 1780, he could write to Washington that he could now walk and ride again. "In other respects I am in perfect health and even enjoy the comforts and pleasures of life with as good a relish as most of my neighbors." Washington replied cordially.

Putnam was determined not to be an invalid. He had a spirited bay mare that he could control perfectly and bring to a dead halt by shaking the knob of his ivory cane. Though he had to be helped into the saddle, he rode out each day, often accompanied by Dick, the ex-slave he had rescued in Havana, to visit sons and daughters and friends. In the autumn of 1780 he rode to Tappan on the Hudson for a visit with army friends and a few years later to visit his brother in Danvers.

So he settled into a life that was full and social. No man was ever a better companion, and after the war was over the stream of visitors increased; old comrades and new friends would sit by the hour with him reminiscing of men and battles. No occasion, from a barn raising to a wedding, was complete without the General in an armchair surrounded by a laughing crowd of children and friends. Religion grew in importance in his life: on Sundays he went to church services and evening prayer meetings and took part in church affairs.

One visitor was his former aide, David Humphreys, who spent several months talking with the General and making notes of the events of his life, which he remembered with clarity and detail. Later, while visiting Washington at Mount Vernon, Humphreys wrote the first biography of Putnam, published in 1788. At the close he said, "He seems to have been formed on purpose for the age in which he lived. His native courage, unshaken integrity and established reputation as a soldier were necessary in the early stages of our opposition to the designs of Great Britain and gave unbounded confidence to our troops in their first appearance on the field of battle."

Late in May, 1790, he was attacked by an "inflamatory disease." On the 29th, Major General Israel Putnam, citizen, patriot, soldier, died in his 73rd year.

For more than 20 years he had been a symbol to the people of New England, an oak tree standing squarely to face whatever the winds of fortune brought. A citizen, he had never hesitated to go to fight for his country whenever and wherever needed. A soldier, he had never hesitated to lead his men into the fight, nor to treat them and their enemies afterwards with kindness. A patriot, he had worked mightily for liberty and justice for all.

So Israel Putnam appears on the pages of history as the right man on the right spot at the right time. Before the war, by his energy and devotion to the cause of liberty and freedom he had helped prepare the people of Connecticut for the struggle to come. In the earliest days, before there was a recognized war, the citizen-turned-soldier had needed the assurance that the sight of a famous citizen, also turned soldier, could give, and the comfort that came from the knowledge that an important man had left his home and family and livelihood because freedom and liberty were more important. Putnam was just such a man as the New England militia come to the siege of Boston understood and valued because he understood and valued them, and because he did not hold himself above them, they put him above them.

By the very force of his character, his integrity, his unswerving devotion to his country, his optimism and his energy and vitality, he could arouse the same qualities in the men under him. If his compassion for the helpless was scorned and misinterpreted, his generosity of spirit allowed him to ignore those who decried him. There was no jealousy in his nature, and no meanness of spirit, even when he was blamed for the errors of others. And whatever he did, he did with all his might. His simplicity, modesty, and friendliness, his whole stalwart character, were perhaps not understood and appreciated by men from other parts of the country. But he bestrode his own world like a colossus, and his people respected and loved him.

And so as a symbol as well as a man he emerges from the mists, galloping his white horse for help for the men on Breed's Hill and stalking behind the men at the rail fence, encouraging the retreating troops up Manhattan again and again to find that extra strength to march a little farther, doing his duty and staying behind in Philadelphia when the army moved on Trenton. He was one of the last of the old-fashioned type of soldier and patriot of whom his country can be most proud.

The inscription on his gravestone was composed by Dr. Timothy Dwight, soon to become President of Yale College. It included the famous words "Who . . . Dared to lead Where any Dared to Follow."

To the memory
Of
Israel Putnam, Esquire,
Senior Major-General in the Armies
Of
The United States of America
Who
Was born at Salem
In the Province of Massachusetts
On the seventh day of January
A.D. 1718
And died
On the twenty ninth day of May
A.D. 1790:

Passenger
If thou art a Soldier
Drop a Tear over the Dust of a Hero
Who
Ever Attentive
To the lives and happiness of his Men
Dared to lead
Where any Dared to Follow;
If a Patriot
Remember the distinguished and gallant services
rendered thy Country
By the Patriot who sleeps beneath this Monument;
If thou art Honest, generous and worthy

Render a cheerful tribute of respect
To a Man
Whose generosity was singular
Whose honesty was proverbial
Who
Raised himself to universal esteem
And offices of Eminent distinction
By personal worth
And a
Useful life.